THE PROBLEM WITH PENGUINS

The Problem with Penguins

Stand Out in a Crowded Marketplace by Packaging Your BIG Idea

Bill Bishop

iUniverse, Inc.
New York   Bloomington

The Problem with Penguins
Stand Out in a Crowded Marketplace
by Packaging Your BIG Idea

iUniverse books may be ordered through booksellers or by contacting:

iUniverse
1663 Liberty Drive
Bloomington, IN 47403
www.iuniverse.com
1-800-Authors (1-800-288-4677)

ISBN: 978-1-4502-1204-5 (pbk)
ISBN: 978-1-4502-1202-1 (cloth)
ISBN: 978-1-4502-1203-8 (ebook)

Printed in the United States of America

iUniverse rev. date: 3/3/2010

Praise for Bill's book How To Sell A Lobster

My husband and I really enjoyed your book. So much excellent advice in such a complete package! We are impressed! But we must know: "Who is Marketing Mike? Please reveal the mystery! Thanks for improving our business!
Jamie and Kelly

My name is Taseo. I am a third year BBA student. I have just finished reading your book *How To Sell A Lobster* and I can honestly say I learned more about marketing than in my recent 5 month marketing course. The material was simple to digest which was a real treat for me since it is a big change from overly wordy and flat out boring marketing text books. I just wanted to thank you for writing this book and allowing me to share the experience you've gained in the marketing world.
Taseo

I have just finished reading your book *How To Sell A Lobster*. It was fascinating and I couldn't put it down until I had finished reading it cover to cover. Most of the challenges that were described in your book are exactly the challenges that we are facing as a small company trying to "get off the ground". I am very interested in exploring in more detail how those marketing strategies could be applied to our business.
Pat

Hi, my name is Natalie and I am 12 years old. I read the book *How to Sell A Lobster* and I enjoyed it very much and finished it in only three days! My favorite story was The Line-Up, because

I found it was a very smart way to make customers interested in your business. My mom and I enjoyed your book and we thought it was very funny. My mom thinks that Marketing Mike is you and I am not quite sure. If you could please reply and let us know who Marketing Mike is we would really appreciate it. Thank you.
Natalie

Really enjoyed your book. I am applying some of your ideas to my business. I'll bite, who is Marketing Mike?
Mike

Found that your book *How To Sell A Lobster* was spell binding and I was unable to put it down. So I did not until I finished. One question though: Who is Marketing Mike? We will be trying The Three Boxes in our business presentation. Thank You
Brian & Diana

I have read your book many times since I received it. There is so much information that I can use in my business. Thanks very much for a great book. Now to the question! Who is Marketing Mike? I am very curious. Thanks.
Betty

I just finished your book *How To Sell A Lobster*. It is an absolutely fantastic book! I thoroughly enjoyed every single chapter - each one packed with valuable information, and written in an extremely easy to read writing style! This is definitely one of the most "valuable" books I have read, and I have read a LOT of books over the years! I will definitely be applying it!
Wayne

I have just completed reading your book *How To Sell A Lobster* for the first time. I will guarantee there will be many rereads. It was an extremely interesting and eye-opening experience. I am also glad to learn that you are Canadian. I think it is well overdo that we have some Canadian talent of this quality.

Chris

I gave *How To Sell A Lobster* to my brother-in-law who owns a small bakery. At first he told me he would never read it (he's not a "reader"). I gave it to him anyway. He started reading it and then called me up and couldn't stop raving about how good the book was (gee . . . what a surprise!). He then wanted to find out where he could get more of these books. He wanted to give one to his manager and a few more copies for his business partners. He feels every business owner should read *How To Sell A Lobster*!

Pat

I just read your book *How To Sell A Lobster*, and as a partner in a small consulting firm, I found it enjoyable and insightful. I have also asked my colleagues to read it. I am hopeful that we can apply some of the learning, as we relate to so many of the examples described. I wanted to take a minute and thank you for sharing the experience.

Khan

Well, Mr. Bishop you've peaked my curiosity. I have just finished *How To Sell A Lobster* and must know, who is Marketing Mike? Besides having a wealth of knowledge and insight into human nature, he must also be one of great generosity to have shared his wisdom so willingly with you. My curiosity is peaked....please tell me who is Marketing Mike?

Poseann

I am reading your book for a second time. Your teaching and techniques are an eye opener and have really stuck with me. At the first time of reading I didn't implement anything so upon reading your book the second time, I put your techniques to work at a yard sale I did and it was amazing how much I sold by giving people a choice, i.e. 1 item for $1 or any 2 for $1.50. I worked with myself to look at what I was doing as marketing items I no longer needed and someone else did. I am looking forward to utilizing your teaching in other areas of my life and helping my grown children as well.

Irene

Where were you three years ago? I have been struggling to keep my head above water in this business (which I love very much) but it's tough. The "Lobster" book was excellent.

Lucio

I just finished reading your book *How To Sell A Lobster*. Great read! And I must say, I love the ideas and mind set you create. I am fascinated by many of the principles your book *How To Sell A Lobster* defines/shares. And as an actor, I am trying to apply these principles to what I do and my career.

David

I read your book and loved it. Every word, every page...

Shelly

My name is Olga. I am from Ufa, the big city in the middle of Russia. I decided to write this letter with words of gratitude for your book *How To Sell A Lobster*. When I took this small book in my hands in a bookshop firstly I was not impressed much but I decided to buy it. I was very surprised. I found all advice from the book very useful for my retail business. Especially I was impressed with an advice "Three Boxes". Now, when a customer is in my coffee-tea boutique, my seller asks him: "How much of product do you want to buy: 100, 150 or 200 grams?" And 8 from 10 customers usually answer "150", and sometimes "200"! Although the minimum volume of purchase is 50 grams. Other advice also useful. For example, the advice about "box of chocolate". We made mini-pockets with tea (just for a one cup) and now offer them to vacillating customers with floor prices. And often these people come back to our boutique to buy bigger volume of tea. So I would like to tell thank you very much for your book *How To Sell A Lobster*.

Olga

I read your book (the Romanian translation) in couple of hours after my wife bought it. I was happy and nervous in the same time. Happy because I saw in Marketing Mike someone that I have been for most of my friends and most of my employers (if they were smart enough to listen), and nervous to see that I did not consider doing from this as a business.

Razvan

I wanted to take this opportunity to congratulate you on your success. Amongst all the glitter and clutter of business books in the market, it's comforting to find a message that speaks clearly to small businesses and delivers real applicable concepts that are adaptable to the entrepreneurs of the world. I recently ordered 5 copies of your book, *How To Sell A Lobster,* through Amazon. ca. I feel it's the perfect gift for some of my small business clients who struggle to grasp some of the key marketing concepts that could propel their endeavors to the next level of success. Your presentation methods are classic, simple and most of all direct, enabling you to reach your audience on a deeper level. I've read through my copy six or seven times and keep coming back for reminders. Keep up the good work and I look forward to your upcoming releases.

Joey

To order *How To Sell A Lobster*, visit amazon.com or call 416.364.8770.

To Beverly and Jim

For teaching me that
the delusion of self
stops every penguin from achieving real happiness

FROM THE AUTHOR OF
The Problem With Penguins

Books

Strategic Marketing For The Digital Age
Grow Your Business With Online and Digital Technology

Global Marketing For The Digital Age
How To Expand Your Business in The Global Marketplace
Using Advanced Digital Technology

The Strategic Enterprise
Growing A Business For The 21st Century

How To Sell A Lobster
The Money-Making Secrets of A Streetwise Entrepreneur

Educational CD/Booklets

Packaging The Invisible Box

How To Create A Marketing Plan That Works

The 25 Packaging Mistakes and How To Avoid Them

The 13 BIG Idea Strategies

The Last Goal

The Transformation Economy

The Publishing Success Solution

*Visit www.BishopBigIdeas.com
for all of Bill's latest creations*

Contents

PART THREE: PACKAGING YOUR BIG IDEA

PART FOUR: SELLING YOUR BIG IDEA

PART FIVE: THERE MUST BE SOME KIND OF WAY OUT OF HERE

PART SIX: TOOLS FOR PENGUINS IN RECOVERY

Preface

4,000 Big Ideas & Counting

During the past 25 years working as a business coach, speaker, writer and the CEO of Bishop Communications Inc., I've learned a lot about sales and marketing, but one lesson stands out as pre-eminent. If you want to be successful in business, you need a Big Idea—something new, better and different—that gets the attention of your prospects and makes you stand out from your competition. Without a Big Idea, your strategies and tactics may not work no matter how well executed. That's because your idea is either boring, generic, or similar to products and services offered by your competition.

That's why I created my program *The BIG Idea Adventure*. It's a methodical step-by-step process that helps companies, entrepreneurs, and salespeople create, package and sell new BIG Ideas. Our coaches love guiding people through this process because we see instant results. When the light goes on, and they come up with their Big Idea, our members get really excited and re-commit to the success of their business. We've also witnessed other incredible results. Armed with their Big Idea, the members of our program make more sales, and take home a lot more money. Some have made millions. They also do many new wonderful things that make the world a better place.

Since we created the program more than 4,000 companies across North America and around the world have experienced the joy of the Big Idea. I hope this book will do the same for you. (To learn more, visit www.BishopBigIdeas.com)

Introduction

The Problem With Penguins

Not long ago, I saw a fascinating movie called *March of The Penguins*. Perhaps you've seen it. The movie is about penguins in Antarctica. Every few years, they march 75 miles to the same breeding ground their ancestors have been using for millions of years.

Watching the movie, I was intrigued by one particular scene showing thousands of penguins huddling together for warmth. I was struck by the fact that all of the penguins look exactly the same. You can't tell one from the other. In fact, the penguins have a difficult time telling each other apart. The penguins even look the same to the other penguins!

Watching the movie, it occurred to me that most business people have the same problem. They look just like their competitors. They sell the same kinds of products and services. They tell the same stories. They do the same things. Sure, there might be a few subtle differences, but from the perspective of the marketplace, through the eyes of their prospects, they all look like a bunch of penguins.

Dealing with this penguin problem is important because you need to do something big and dramatic if you want to stand out in today's over-crowded and competitive marketplace. Everyday, there are more and more penguins entering your industry, and they all look like you. Go on the Internet and enter the name

If you sell the same things as your competitors, and do basically the same things, it is very difficult for you to stand out in a crowded marketplace, and make a quantum leap in growth.

of your product or service on Google. How many search results did you get? I tried it for the words "financial advisor" and I got 28,700,000 results. 28,700,000! And that's just the financial advisors who have a web site.

If you want to make more money, the penguin problem is a big obstacle. If your prospects view you and your competitors as exactly the same, they will choose the supplier with the lowest possible price. That means: even if you get the business, you won't make much of a profit.

If you want to attract more great prospects, the penguin problem is also a big obstacle. If you look and sound like everyone else, why would your prospects want to meet with you? They don't want to hear the same old thing they've heard a hundred times before. They want to hear something new, better, and different.

The penguin problem is also a roadblock if you want to grow your business. If you sell essentially the same things as your competitors, and do basically the same things, it will be very difficult to make a quantum leap in growth. That's because, with few barriers to entry, your industry will keep getting more crowded with penguins. Supply will become greater than demand, and your growth will stall or even fall.

That's why the penguin problem is something you need to deal with.

It's also important to realize that the penguin problem is new. In the old days, you could be a penguin and still make a good living. Years ago, nobody had a lot of competition. In the 1960's for example, my mom and dad ran a public relations company. They only had a handful of competitors, and there was more than enough business to go around. They didn't have to worry about standing out. There was more demand than supply.

But today things are much different. Your industry has become jam packed with penguins. They're marching into your marketplace across international borders and over the Internet. They're also converging on you from other industries. Lawyers are becoming financial advisors. Computer makers are becoming entertainment companies. Coffee shops are selling music CDs. Every day, your cozy little ice flow is getting more and more crowded with other penguins all chasing the same customers.

Reading this, you might be thinking: We're not penguins. We're completely different from our competition. That's probably true. But the question is: Can your prospects tell you apart from the other penguins? Can they see quickly that you're not the same as all the rest? After all, every penguin is a unique creature, with different thoughts, feelings, and abilities. But no one can see it. That's because their packaging is the same as the other penguins.

That's why I wrote this book. I want to help you stand out from the other penguins. Otherwise, you could waste hundreds of hours, spend thousands or millions of dollars, and expend lots of energy doing sales and marketing activities that don't work because you haven't addressed the penguin problem.

In this book, I'll explain why you need to develop a *BIG Idea*—something new, better, and different—that will dramatically differentiate you from the other penguins. I'll teach you how to come up with your BIG Idea, and then show you how to brand, package, and promote it. I'll also tell you about dozens of BIG Ideas that have been packaged and sold successfully by our clients over the past 20 years.

One important note: This book is for business people who want to take action, and get things done. You might have read books on this subject such as Blue Ocean Strategy or Purple Cow or worked with a coach who talked conceptually about branding and packaging, but this book is different. It explains step-by-step exactly what you need to do to get your BIG Idea to market quickly so you can start attracting more new customers, making more money, and growing your business as soon as possible.

So if you're finally ready to break away from all those other pesky penguins, read on.

PART ONE

Getting Off The Ice Floe

Chapter 1

The Manchurian Marketer:
Why BIG Idea Penguins Are A Rare Bird

To stand out from the other penguins, you need a BIG Idea. Not just any idea, a really BIG Idea. It's not enough to be different, you have to be a lot different.

Think about it this way. Let's say the temperature in your room is 72 degrees Fahrenheit, and someone turns up the heat to 73 degrees. That is a different temperature, but do you notice it? Probably not. There isn't enough of a difference.

Many business people make this mistake. They do something different, but it's only a little bit different. They change the color of their product or they offer improved credit terms. But these additions and changes aren't enough. To the untrained eye, they still look like the other penguins.

But what if someone increased the temperature to 90 degrees? Would you notice the difference? Of course you would. It would be a lot hotter! You'd start sweating, you'd take off your sweater and say: "Hey, who turned up the temperature? It's boiling in here."

So that's what you need to do. If you want people to notice you, you need to turn up the heat, and do something really different. That's what I call a BIG Idea.

Being Brainwashed: Coming up with a BIG Idea can be tough, but not for the reasons you might think. It's not because you lack creativity or imagination. It's not because you're not smart. It's because you're brainwashed. You've been brainwashed to think first about your products and services.

Not convinced? Take this simple test. Write down your elevator speech. What do you say if someone asks about your business? Keep it to one or two sentences. Now read it out loud. Is it about your products or services? Typically, people say something like: "I'm a financial advisor" or "I'm a dentist" or "We sell computers." They tell you about their product or service.

But what else would you say? It seems logical to tell people about your products and services because that's what you do. But it's a problem because the other penguins in your industry are telling exactly the same elevator speech about their products and services. That's why no one can tell you apart from the other penguins. Not only do you look alike, you also sound alike.

But there's an even bigger problem. It's not just what you say, it's also how you think. When you think about your business, you always think first about your product or service. That's always the starting point. So when you try to come up with a BIG Idea—something new, better or different—it's really hard because your brain always starts with your product or service.

You then think about how to make your product bigger, smaller, faster, slower, prettier. These efforts aren't a total waste of time—it's always good to make your product better—but typically the changes are small ones—like turning up the temperature to 73 degrees. It's not enough. You still look like the other penguins.

You could try to get your BIG Idea from other penguins. You could go to conferences and learn from other people in your industry. If someone has a good idea, you could copy it. There is nothing wrong with that either, except it won't help you with the penguin problem. Most of the ideas you will get from other penguins will be small incremental ideas of the 73 degree variety. In addition, copying what other penguins are already doing doesn't put you ahead of the curve, and help you stand out as unique. It just makes you a follower.

So how do you break out of this trap? How do you stop thinking first about your products and services, and come up with a unique Big Idea?

You begin by thinking about someone else—namely your customer. I know this sounds radical, but it works. Instead of thinking first about you and your products/services, you turn things around and think first about your customers.

That probably sounds like the most obvious advice ever. You're thinking: "I bought this book and that's all I get? Think about my customers first? What a rip-off!" But hold on, it's not as easy as you think because you've been brainwashed and you don't know it. And before you protest, keep in mind that one of the sure signs of brainwashing is that the victim doesn't know they've been brainwashed.

Do you remember the movie *The Manchurian Candidate*? It's about a candidate for president who has been brainwashed by bad guys to kill another candidate for president. It's a creepy movie. But the key point is: He doesn't know he is brainwashed. He doesn't know he is following instructions programmed into his brain by someone else.

Everyday I meet business people who have been brainwashed by 200 years of the industrial revolution. Their bodies are living in the 21st Century, but their brains are programmed for the 19th Century, and they don't know it!

If your thinking begins with your product or service, it is hard to come up with Big Ideas to stand out from the other penguins in your industry.

Since the beginning of the 19th Century, business has been all about products and services. To succeed, you followed a simple formula. Think of a product. Build a machine to make it. Then sell the product.

It was easy. Think of product. Build a machine to make it. Sell the product. Make a lot of money. Buy a big house. Hire servants.

Lots of people got rich following this formula. Then they applied it to services. Think of a service. Build a machine to deliver it. (A machine made of people this time). Sell the service. Make a lot of money. Buy a big house. Hire servants.

For two hundred years, this formula worked. One generation passed on the formula to the next. They said, "Son (or Daughter), if you want to get rich, follow this formula. Think of a product or service. Build a machine to make it. Sell this product or service. Make a lot of money. Buy a big house. Hire servants." What could be easier?

And then people stopped saying it out loud. The formula was so successful and so well known that no one needed to say it anymore. It was what it was—a universal truth. At that point, everyone's brains were fully washed.

But then the world changed. Someone invented the personal computer, and then the World Wide Web. Trade barriers fell and we had a global economy. Regulations that kept industries separate from each other were eliminated. The market was flooded with more and more competitors.

This increase in competition made it essential to come up with a BIG Idea, but the brainwashing made it hard because everyone started with step one of the old formula: think of a product or service—which made it almost impossible to come up with something that hadn't been done already.

In the old days, if you made a product—let's say bobby pins—you were the only person making them. So you had the market to yourself. You could just keep running the machine day and night, year after year, making the same bobby pins. In no time, you were living in the big house getting waited on by servants.

But eventually, other people living in little houses with no servants pulled together enough money to build their own machines, and they started making bobby pins too. Suddenly, you had competition. Then people in other countries got in the bobby pin business. They hired people to work dirt cheap. So the price of bobby pins dropped and dropped.

Afraid you might have to sell the house and let go of the servants, you looked for another product. You considered zippers. But there were already two hundred companies in the zipper market. What about lava lamps? No, that was a crowded market too. How about mouse pads? No, same problem. Everywhere you looked, other penguins had beaten you to it.

My point is this: The world has changed. There are a lot of penguins out there, and if you want to come up with a BIG Idea that is a lot different, you have to use a new thinking process. If you don't de-program yourself, and cast off 200 years of product-first thinking, it will be extremely hard for you to come up with a BIG Idea. The old product-first mindset will simply smother your creativity.

Apple is a great example of a company that de-programmed itself. For two decades the company enjoyed a modest level of success with its fantastic computers (I'm a Mac user from day one). But for those 20 years, it was a small player in the overall computer market. But one day, Steve Jobs and his team broke away from product-first (computer-first) thinking, and started focusing first on their customer. When they made that simple change in perspective, they had lots of amazing Big Ideas— namely iTunes, the iPod and the iPhone—which dramatically increased their sales and differentiated them from the other computer companies. The key lesson is: If Apple had stay mired in product-first thinking, they would have never come up with these innovations. The ironic thing is: By creating and selling Big Ideas—that don't look anything like computers—they now also sell a lot more computers.

So let's learn from the former penguins at Apple. If you want to turn up the temperature to 90 degrees, and come up with something really hot, forget about your products and services— even forget about your industry— and begin your thinking with a new starting point: namely, your #1 Customer Type.

Chapter 2

No More Egg Rolls:
Getting Focused on Your #1 Customer Type

Most business owners have too many different kinds of customers. They sell their products and services to anyone. For example, they might sell their widgets to dog catchers, family doctors, and sanitation workers. It doesn't matter to them who the customer is as long as they sell something.

But this lack of focus is a big problem for them. For one thing, they spread themselves too thin. They try to play too many games at once. It's like they try to play hockey and football at the same time. It's confusing and difficult. They also never become a specialist in the eyes of their customers: They look like a jack of all trades. They look like the Chinese restaurant that advertises tax return services in the window. You can munch on egg rolls while they work out your tax refund. It's just a little nutty.

But there's a bigger problem. Having too many different kinds of customers means you don't really know any of your customers very well. You're just selling stuff. You aren't investigating your market in detail. You're not thinking about what your customers might need that isn't being offered in the marketplace. As such, it's unlikely you will come up with a Big Idea.

So you need to get focused. You need to decide whom you really want to work with. In our case, we decided years ago that

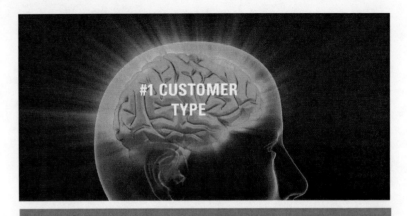

If you make your #1 Customer Type the focus of your thinking, it will be easier for you to come up with Big Ideas.

we wanted to work with entrepreneurs, specifically small business owners and salespeople. We didn't want to work anymore with large corporations, associations, or the government.

That was the best decision we ever made. Since that time, we've worked with thousands of business owners and salespeople in dozens of industries. We've become experts in helping them get more customers and make more money. This focus on our #1 Customer Type has given us an in-depth understanding of entrepreneurs: their goals and special challenges. This understanding has enabled us to come up with dozens of BIG Ideas that have been very profitable.

So who is your #1 Customer Type?

To figure it out, make a list of all your different kinds of customers and then choose the best one. What type of customer do you love working with? Which one is the most enjoyable and the most profitable? Which ones don't you like working with? Eliminate them from your list.

Decidedly, it isn't easy at first to focus on just one type of customer. It's hard to give up the others. You think you're giving up opportunities. But in fact, the opposite is true. We have a client—a financial advisor—who decided to work exclusively with dentists. At the time he had about five dentists. Now he has over 300. By focusing on dentists, he was able to develop some great BIG Ideas, and was able to put all of his marketing time and money into one market. Now he is seen as the number one financial advisor for dentists.

Take your time with this decision. It's the most important decision you'll ever make in your business.

Chapter 3

The Gourmet Penguin:
Make More Money Selling An Up-Scale Package

Would you like to charge more for your products and services? I'm sure you would. But maybe you think your customers won't pay more. Maybe you're afraid your customers will walk away and do business with your lower-priced competitors.

This is a natural fear, but it doesn't get you anywhere. If you're afraid to charge more, then you never will. And if you never do it, you will be stuck where you are. In fact, it's likely you will make less and less money as time goes by as increasing competition puts the squeeze on your prices and profit margins.

So how can you get out of this trap? How can you charge more without losing any customers? Better yet, how can you increase your prices and grow your customer base at the same time?

Before I give you my strategy for increasing prices, it's important to understand what I call *The Wal-Mart Effect*. We all know that Wal-Mart promises the lowest prices possible. They have built a worldwide empire on this promise. But these low prices are a mixed blessing. Although some consumers benefit from the bargains at Wal-Mart, small retailers are often driven out of business because they can't compete.

It is doubly sad because many of these retailers don't need to go out of business. They simply need to change their business, and

To stand out, offer your prospects two choices: the typical fast food sold by your competitors, and a gourmet option only sold by you.

do what Wal-Mart can't do: which is to provide a gourmet service. They need to provide a higher level of service, experience, and value than Wal-Mart. In other words, they need to stop trying to compete with Wal-Mart on price, and do something Wal-Mart can't do: They need to become gourmet retailers instead.

You might be thinking: That's fine, but I'm not in a retail business. Yes, but *The Wal-Mart Effect* is happening in every industry. Driven by e-commerce and globalization, companies in every industry are developing ways to deliver products and services over the Internet for the lowest prices possible. I call these Fast Food companies.

Many companies go crazy trying to compete with the Fast Food competitors in their industry. They think the only way is to lower their prices. But if they lower their prices they won't make a profit. So it's a Catch 22.

Thankfully there is a way out. They need to become Gourmet companies. They need to package BIG Ideas that take everything to higher level. And they need to charge a lot more money for this gourmet meal.

For example, let's say you have an insurance agency. You have watched while insurance carriers and banks have gone online to sell insurance directly to the public. They sell insurance products just like yours for lower prices. Customers simply fill out an online application and bingo: They get a policy.

You've thought about going online too, but you can't make it work. The upfront investment is huge, and your online competitors are much bigger, and much better capitalized.

So instead of chasing the Fast Food competition, I suggest you make a 180 degree turn, and become a Gourmet company. You develop a special program, for example, called *The Safe & Sound Solution*. You offer this program to your best customers, and charge $1,200. For this fee, you spend a lot of time with your clients to make sure they have identified all of their risks, and have an overall plan to protect themselves. You also photograph and assess the value of all their possessions in case they need to make a claim in the future. The program delivers significantly more value than any of your competitors are willing to provide for free.

The great thing is: Your customers won't say you are charging too much, and your new $1,200 program won't scare them away. That's because your program is simply an upscale option. You tell them you have two levels of service: fast food and gourmet. You can provide either a simple insurance transaction or they can hire you for the $1,200 gourmet package. It is up to them to choose what they want: fast food or gourmet.

It's like you are running a hotel. You have 400 nice, reasonably-priced rooms. Then you add 40 penthouse suites on the top of the hotel. You now tell people you have both regular and super-deluxe rooms. It is up to them to decide.

Of course you might think no one will opt for the penthouse suites. Perhaps, but you will never know until you try. Many business owners discover there is a pent-up demand for the gourmet package because their customers haven't been completely satisfied with the fast food, or they have outgrown it.

Moreover, there is no risk with this approach. Unlike the hotel, you can probably develop the gourmet service with little or no upfront investment. You can then offer it in addition to your regular services. The best part is: If your customers want the gourmet package, you make more money. But if they don't want to pay the higher price, they can always become a customer anyway and buy the fast food. You see, there is no risk. There is no danger of losing a potential customer by offering your gourmet package.

But there is a risk if you don't offer a gourmet package. If one of your competitors creates a better, more upscale offering, some of your best customers might jump ship and start working with them. That would be ironic wouldn't it? You are afraid to charge more because you think you might lose a customer, but in fact, you might lose a customer if you don't charge more.

Remember, not everyone is looking for the lowest price. Do you drive the cheapest car on the market? Do you eat in the cheapest restaurants? Do you wear cheap second-hand clothes? Probably not. So why do you think all of your customers want the cheapest price? You might be pleasantly surprised to discover that many of your customers want to pay more, sometimes a lot more. (Later I will explain the benefits of providing a third, super-gourmet offer.)

So the strategy to charge more and make more money is simple. Package a gourmet BIG Idea. Offer it in addition to your existing fast food products and services. And charge a lot of money for it.

Chapter 4

Turning The Tables:
Getting More Ideal Customers Knocking On Your Door

Most penguins will work with customers who are, shall we say, less than ideal?

You know the type of customer. They don't take your relationship seriously. They waste your time. They're demanding. They grumble about your invoices. They don't pay on time. They miss appointments or show up late. They don't respect your experience and expertise.

Let's face it. You can't stand them. But you keep working with them. Why? Because you believe you have to work with everyone: that it will be financial suicide to turn away any customer relationship: no matter how odious or retrograde to your self-esteem.

Most penguins are slaves. They're slaves to customers who think, because they are paying money, that they can treat their suppliers like second-class citizens. But you didn't start your company to be a slave. You want freedom.

That's why you have to change the game, and assert your power as a free and independent person. You have to stop being a slave, and turn the tables on your prospects and customers. This is another benefit that can be achieved by packaging.

If you don't want to be a slave anymore, here's what I recommend. When explaining your new gourmet BIG Idea, tell

If you tell your prospects that your gourmet Big Idea is not for everyone, they will want it more, and even line up for it.

your prospects it's a special thing that's "not for everyone." That's it. Just tell them it's not for everyone.

So how will this help you break the bonds of customer-enslavement?

For starters, it's important to note there is one thing people want more than anything else. No it's not more money, or a bigger house, or a better car. Those things are nice, but the thing people want more than anything else is *something they might not be able to get.*

It's just human nature. When people think they might not be able to get something—either now or in the future—they grab for it, even if they don't really know what it is, or whether they really want it. In their mind, it's just safer to grab it and then figure out the details later.

Here's an example. Twenty years ago, my tennis club had a waiting list of 200 people who wanted to become members. This positioned the club as very exclusive and "hard-to-get-into." The image of exclusivity made people want in and bolstered the size of the waiting list. It also made it easier to close people on the waiting list because they were afraid if they didn't act at that moment, they would lose their place in line, and then maybe they would never get to become a member. It was a dream scenario for the membership director.

But then the bottom fell out of the economy and more clubs opened in the city. Now the waiting list is gone and the club is begging people to join. Without a waiting list, the club looks less exclusive and less desirable. It's also harder to close prospects because they know they don't have to make up their mind right away. They can wait and still get in later. This is a nightmare scenario for the membership director.

This impulse is part of our hoarding instinct. We tend to value things more if we're afraid we won't be able to get them in the future.

Here's an interesting example. Years ago, I had a favorite cereal that was hard to find. Most of the time, when I went to the grocery store, it was out of stock. If it was in stock, I would grab as many boxes as I could because I was afraid I might not be able to get it in the future. But then I realized why the product was so often out of stock. Other people were hoarding it for the same reason. This perpetual cycle of scarcity led to a hoarding market for this type of cereal. (Alas, eventually the company discontinued the cereal, forcing me to now ingest lesser cereals at breakfast.)

That's why I recommend you tell prospects your gourmet BIG Idea is not for everybody. In fact, it's not for most people. When you say this, your prospects will worry they might not be able to get into the exclusive club. That will force them to make up their mind right then, not wait until later.

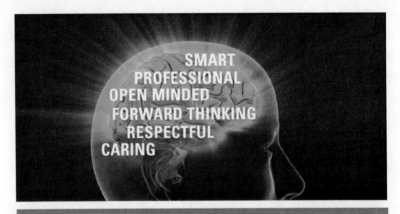

If you help your prospects package their self-image—by giving them words to describe themselves—they will buy your Big Idea as a way to reinforce this self-image.

This strategy is also great because it puts you and your customer on an equal footing. You no longer beg them to work with you. Instead, you decide if you want to work with them.

Packaging Their Self-Image

Another related packaging technique that works extremely well is helping your prospects package and reinforce their own self-image. These are the words they use to describe to themselves who they really are, or more precisely, who they want to be. It is one of the most important and powerful marketing techniques ever invented.

Begin by articulating the characteristics of your ideal customer. For example, you might say your ideal customer is smart, open-minded, forward-thinking, and someone who respects and values the advice of a professional.

Then use these words to make your program even more exclusive. Say: "My new gourmet program is not for anyone. It's only for people who are smart, open-minded, forward thinking, and for someone who respects and values the advice of professionals. If you are someone like that, you might be interested in this new gourmet program. If not, don't worry, I can still sell you the fast food."

What kind of reaction will you get, do you think, if you present your gourmet program in this manner? My experience reveals that people respond very positively. They want to believe they are that kind of person. They don't want to think, or admit, they are the opposite: stupid, close-minded, backward thinking, and someone who doesn't respect or value the advice of a professional. Few people want to believe they are like that.

By using these words, you help your prospect "package" their self-image. Now they have words to describe themselves to themselves. Psychological experiments have shown that when people have packaged their self-image, they will then make a big effort to prove to themselves, and to others, that this self-image is true. That's when they will say: "Yes, that sounds like me. I'm not fast food. I'm gourmet. Tell me about your new gourmet program. It sounds like something I need."

Helping prospects package their self-image is what all sophisticated marketers do. Why do you think advertising usually shows beautiful people doing wonderful happy things? It's because it helps people create a picture of their desired self-image. A woman sees a model in a fashion magazine and says: "That's who I want to be." Then she goes out and spends $400 on a perm, buys $100 lipsticks, and plunks down $3,000 for a Prada purse. A man sees an ad with a great looking guy driving a BMW sports car. The guy says: "That's me. That's who I want to be." So he goes out and spends $80,000 on a BMW.

The point is: by telling your prospects your gourmet program is not for everyone, and by telling them they must have certain characteristics to qualify, they will make a psychological shift.

They will no longer see you as a subservient supplier they can order around. They will see you as a professional who can help them achieve and reinforce a very positive self-image.

Most importantly, by turning the tables, you'll stand out from the other penguins in your industry. You will be doing something different from the other salespeople in your industry. Unlike you, they knock on doors. They beg prospects to work with them, and they sell fast food. Their methods, because they are the same as everyone else, make them a bunch of penguins.

But you will stand out by doing things differently. You will tell prospects about your gourmet package, and then tell them it isn't for everybody. Then you will wait for them to come to you. Remember, the one thing people want more than anything else is something they fear they might not be able to get. They also want to reinforce a positive self-image.

Keep in mind that this technique works because it reflects the true reality of your situation. What you are selling is not for everyone, because whatever it is, most people won't buy it. Imagine if you went out on the street and gave away free $100 bills. Do you think everyone would take them? Probably not. Some people will refuse because they will think there is a catch or something. So even free $100 bills are not for everyone. That's why this technique is great. It makes a virtue of the fact that most people won't buy your product.

One last point. This advice is not for everybody. Most business owners, marketers and salespeople are too afraid to turn people away. They will keep trying to get everyone to buy from them, and they will keep using the same old sales techniques.

This approach is only for people who are gutsy, patient, psychologically-minded, and willing to try new things. So, if you are someone like that, then this advice is for you. If not, that's okay, you can keep being a penguin.

PART TWO:

Creating Your Big Idea

Chapter 5

Being John Malkovich:
See The World Through Your Customer's Eyes

Most penguins are self-absorbed. They won't admit it, but they only see the world through their eyes. Even if they wanted to, they wouldn't know how to see the world through the eyes of their customers. It's one of the major reasons why most penguins don't stand out in a crowd or make a lot of money.

Have you seen the movie *Being John Malkovich* written by Charlie Kaufman? It's one of my favorite movies. It satirizes our ego-centered culture. The main character Craig Shwartz (played by John Cusack) discovers a hole in a wall at his office that transports him into the body and mind of John Malkovich. When Schwartz goes through this portal he sees the world through the eyes of John Malkovich. It's hilarious.

My favorite scene in the movie is when John Malkovich himself goes through the portal. All the people look like John Malkovich, and everyone keeps saying: "Malkovich, Malkovich, Malkovich." With this scene, Kaufman is saying that most of us are not only self-centered, but that we take it one step further, and project ourselves—our fears, desires, and emotions—onto everyone else. In psychological terms, this is called projection.

Penguins are masters of projection. They love talking about themselves and their products, and they think everyone loves hearing their stories. They live in a fictionalized world where every prospect is just a projection of them.

Poor penguins. They fail to realize their prospects don't care about them and their products. Their prospects don't want to work with them because they think they're boring and self-absorbed. That's why most penguins don't sell very much or make a lot of money. They don't know how to see the world through the eyes of their customers. They're being John Malkovich.

It's obvious. If you don't want to be a penguin, you need to see the world through the eyes of your customers. You need to think what your customers are thinking, and feel what your customers are feeling. But how do you do it? Is there some kind of portal you can go through?

The Titanic Technique

I wish I had a portal, it would be so much easier, but I don't. But I do have a technique you can use called *The Titanic Technique*. Imagine selling your new gourmet package; something new, better, and different, that takes everything to the next level. You tell prospects that this new special thing is not for everyone. Then imagine you already have 100 or 200 ideal customers who have purchased your new, special thing.

Now imagine further that you are meeting with a prospect. She is ideal. You take her through your step-by-step marketing process and it looks like she is going to sign on as a customer. But then her phone rings and she learns a car hit her dog. Distraught, she apologizes and rushes out the door. You never see her again.

Reflecting on this unexpected turn of events you are disappointed but not much. After all, you already have 200 great customers. But you're concerned about the woman. You know some very bad things could happen to her because she didn't do your special thing. What are those bad things?

I call this approach *The Titanic Technique* because, to answer this question, I want you to pretend your prospect is the captain of the Titanic, and you are trying to sell her lifeboats. Like the penguin that you are, you talk about the features of the lifeboats: They're bigger, lighter, and faster to deploy. But the captain isn't interested. Why? Because she thinks she has an unsinkable ship. (Note: My wife Ginny just commented that if the captain of the Titanic had been a woman, she would have never hit the iceberg. But we will leave that discussion for another book.)

Stonewalled by the captain, you try to put yourself in her place: What bad things could happen to the captain if she doesn't buy your lifeboats? Well let's see: her boat could hit an iceberg, there wouldn't be enough lifeboats, and then 1,800 people would die, including her. Not to mention that, one day, Hollywood would produce a blockbuster movie with Leonardo DiCaprio and Kate Winslet that makes her look like an idiot.

So your first job is to realize that your customers are not usually very interested in hearing about the features of your products or the technicalities. To get their attention and keep it, you need to make your story about them, not about you. You also need to convince them that their boat could sink, and that's why they need your lifeboats.

It's like you are driving your car and it starts making a clinkedy-clink sound. Immediately, you go to the service station. The mechanic takes a look under the hood and starts telling you about the pistons and the distributor caps. But you don't care. You want to know if your car will be ready by 4 pm so you can take your kid to a soccer game. The mechanic looks at you like you're an idiot. He doesn't realize you're not interested in pistons and distributors. You just want to take your kid to soccer.

That's why you need to think through to the worst case scenario and tell the captain what the ultimate dangers are. Stop talking about life boats and start talking about people drowning. If you do this, you're talking about the captain, not about yourself. Of course, the captain might be in so much denial that you can't help her, but you've got to give it try. After all, you're not just trying to sell lifeboats. You're also trying to save lives.

That's where the shift happens. If you can remember you are trying to save lives, instead of selling lifeboats, you will begin seeing the world through the eyes of your customers. You will stop talking about you and your products, and talk instead about your prospects and their issues. And if you do that, your prospects will listen because you are talking all about them.

Let me repeat that. If you talk to your prospects all about them, they will be interested because you are making the conversation about them, not you. The reason I repeat this seemingly obvious advice is because I want to tell you something that most business writers or pundits never say out loud. (Promise you will keep this between you and me). The fact is that most of your prospects are penguins themselves. Their world revolves around them. So if you want to get more customers and make more money, you need to talk about them because that is their favorite subject.

Chapter 6

The Peak Benefit:
Discover What Your Customers Really Want

A key principle of packaging is to discover and articulate *The Peak Ben*efit. It will make you and your packaged BIG Idea more relevant and interesting to your prospects. For example, let's imagine you run a web site design company. You create amazing web sites with all the bells and whistles. You also do search engine optimization. Your company has even won awards from the national web site design association. In your mind, you are in the web site design business.

When meeting a prospect, you talk about your company's services, your clients, your awards, and of course, you show them all of the great web sites you've done. The prospect is impressed, but for some reason, you don't really connect with him. He leaves your office and you never see him again.

There could be many reasons you never got the business, but it might be because you didn't package and articulate *The Peak Benefit.* You may have failed because you only talked about helping your prospect create a beautiful and functional web site. You also said you would use search engine optimization so the web site would be easily found by prospects searching the web. These are great benefits, but they are not *The Peak Benefit.*

So what do you think is *The Peak Benefit* the prospect was looking for and the web site company didn't package and

Many penguins lose business because they don't focus on **The Peak Benefit** their customers really want and need.

articulate? What was the real reason the customer wanted to create a web site in the first place? If you look at it from the customer's perspective, *The Peak Benefit* is blindingly obvious: He wanted to get more great customers. Sure, he wanted to have a nice looking web site and show up on the first page of Google, but those were just secondary benefits. Getting new customers is *The Peak Benefit* he wanted.

Once again, this seems so self-evident. But it isn't. I talk with thousands of entrepreneurs and very few of them ever talk about *The Peak Benefit* they provide. They get so caught up in the mechanics of what they are doing they totally forget the real purpose of their product or service. They talk about pistons and carburetors when they should be talking about getting little Johnny to the soccer game on time.

Let me give you another example. I worked with the owner of a funeral home. He was a surprisingly jolly and amiable person. He wanted to stand out from all the other penguins in his industry, but he had a mental roadblock. He was stuck on secondary benefits. He talked about his funeral pre-planning services, his large selection of caskets, and the professional and efficient service provided by his staff. This focus on secondary benefits was reflected in his brochure, his website, and other marketing tools. The problem was: his story was all about him and his funeral home: it wasn't about the client.

To switch things around, and discover *The Peak Benefit*, we spent a few hours talking about his clients. We tried to see the world through their eyes. By doing this, we realized his clients were looking for a funeral home that would help them work through the grieving process with dignity. They wanted to carry out the wishes of their departed loved one. But most importantly, they wanted to work with a funeral director they could talk to and express their feelings with. They wanted to feel supported and cared for, not like some cog in a funeral assembly line. They also wanted this caring person to co-ordinate everything.

That was *The Peak Benefit*: The funeral home needed to make the clients feel supported and cared for. It was not just about caskets and flowers and urns. It was about how they made the client feel.

Understanding their *Peak Benefit* helped the funeral home stand out from the other penguins in their industry. They changed their story and all of their marketing material to reflect their caring and supportive service. They put a picture of a client on their brochure (instead of a picture of their building). They also changed their methods. They spent more time helping the clients express their feelings and making them feel more supported and cared for.

This change of perspective also helped the funeral home think differently about their business. By focusing on *The Peak Benefit*, they came up with new ways to help their clients realize that benefit. For example, they streamlined their process to make it faster and easier for the client to arrange the funeral. They also had grief counselors available in case a client wanted to work with one.

So what is *The Peak Benefit* your customers are looking for? Here's a list of examples:

Financial Services

Secondary Benefit: Make money

Peak Benefit: Achieve life dreams

Health Services

Secondary Benefit: Cure disease

Peak Benefit: Enjoy healthy lifestyle

Beauty/Fashion Industry

Secondary Benefit: Look good

Peak Benefit: Feel good about self

Business Consulting

Secondary Benefit: Create business plan

Peak Benefit: Achieve business goals

Pet Food Industry

Secondary Benefit: Tasty pet food

Peak Benefit: Feel good about caring for your pet

Business Software Industry

Secondary Benefit: Enhance efficiency

Peak Benefit: Successful business

Tennis Racquet Industry

Secondary Benefit: Hit the ball harder

Peak Benefit: Win more matches

Packaging *The Peak Benefit* helps you better connect with your customers because you are more relevant to them. Take Hank for example, my photocopy representative. We do not have a very strong connection because he has never realized or packaged his *Peak Benefit*. Hank only talks about himself and his company's photocopiers. He thinks the benefit he provides is photocopies. In fact, from his perspective, our company is in the business of making photocopies. That's why we don't have a connection. Hank doesn't even know what we do: packaging BIG Ideas. He also doesn't know what I'm trying to do: grow my business. That's *The Peak Benefit* I'm trying to achieve. It isn't about making photocopies.

If Hank were to focus on helping me achieve my *Peak Benefit*, I would feel much more connected to him. I would view his services as much more important. I would also see him as a strategic partner rather than an annoying salesperson who comes around every two years to sell me a more expensive photocopier.

He might also start thinking about how I could use his equipment to make money selling new things to my clients. Then I might get excited about buying a bigger, more expensive photocopier. But that's not what Hank does. He focuses on secondary benefits and makes himself irrelevant to me and what I'm trying to do.

The Escape Hatch

Pinpointing *The Peak Benefit* is the escape hatch for every penguin. If you want to stand out, you need to come up with a BIG Idea by thinking beyond secondary benefits. You need to see the world through your customers' eyes. Otherwise, you will be stuck thinking like the other penguins, and you won't be able to make a breakthrough.

But if you focus on your customer's *Peak Benefit*, you will be able to think up lots of BIG Ideas that are much different from the products and services provided by the other penguins in your industry.

So the big question is: What's your customer's *Peak Benefit?*

An additional point: Just so you're clear that I understand *The Peak Benefit* you are trying to achieve by reading this book, I'm going to tell you. You are reading this book because you want to get more customers and make more money. That's your *Peak Benefit.* The secondary benefit is standing out from a crowd of penguins by packaging your BIG Idea. You want to do that so you can get more customers and make more money. Am I not right?

Chapter 7

The Transformation Economy:
Tap Into A Well of Endless BIG Ideas

Most penguins get stuck on their ice floe because they can't think of any new value to provide their customers. They keep selling the same widgets year after year. They might make some improvements to the widget, but it is still widgets, widgets, widgets. As we discussed in chapter one, they have effectively brainwashed themselves. Their brain can only think widgets.

The reason they can't think of any new value to provide is because they look at the whole situation from a very narrow perspective. By just selling widgets, they only help the customer in one particular way. For example, they sell toothpaste to help their customers clean their teeth. They sell life insurance to help their clients protect their family. They sell photocopiers to help their customer make photocopies.

But as we've learned, customers usually have a higher benefit they are looking for: *The Peak Benefit*. They're not just trying to clean their teeth; they're trying to look great. They're not just trying to protect their family, they want peace of mind. They're not just trying to make photocopies; they want their business to be more successful.

When you don't see *The Peak Benefit* as the most important value provided by your business, you stay stuck selling widgets, and leave a lot of money on the table. You completely miss other

If you try to help your customers achieve a "transformation" you will tap into a well of endless BIG Ideas.

incredible opportunities to help your customer achieve their *Peak Benefit*.

That being said, there is one ultimate *Peak Benefit* very few companies ever recognize: it is to help their customers achieve a *Transformation*. This is a transformation from being out of shape in many ways to being in shape in many ways. If you see your company as a Transformation Company, you will tap into a well of endless BIG Ideas.

So how does it work? Begin by imagining you own a fitness club. You opened the club five years ago and charged $750 for an annual membership. You made a good profit for two years until another club opened across the street. The new club had more facilities and only charged $500 for a membership. So you had to add new equipment and space, and lower your membership fees to $500. As a result, your profit margin shrank, and it was harder to get new members. Things got even worse when a third competitor opened and you had to lower your membership fee to $400.

Frustrated and worried, you did some soul searching, and realized that even at $400, you weren't really helping your members achieve their *Peak Benefit*: To live a happier life by becoming healthier and more fit.   You realized many people who joined your club never got into great shape because they didn't have a plan or a process to follow. They also didn't have a coach to keep them on track. They just showed up and fooled around with the equipment.   Some of the more self-disciplined members got into shape, but many other people stopped coming after their initial enthusiasm wore off.   You also realized your members needed to do more than work out. They also needed to eat better and live a healthier lifestyle.   All in all, you realized you were failing at helping your clients realize their *Peak Benefit* because you were looking at your business from a very narrow perspective.

You decided you wanted to create a gourmet program to help your members achieve a transformation. You kept selling your memberships for $400 (the fast food) but you also offered a gourmet program called *The Great Shape Formula* for $4,000. At that price, you knew the program was not for everybody, but you also knew there were many people who really wanted to get in great shape, and they would pay premium dollars to do so.

You developed the program by thinking about all the ways your members were out of shape when they first came to your club. They were typically over-weight. Their muscles were weak. They had poor cardio-vascular capacity. They were stressed. They also had low self-esteem. The list went on and on.

You thought about how they would be in great shape if they did your program. They would be the right weight for their size and build. They would be stronger. They would have optimum

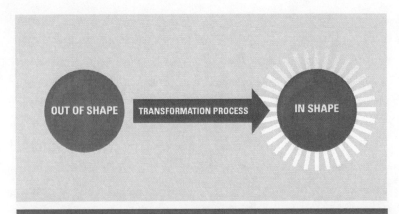

By helping your customers achieve a complete transformation from out-of-shape to in-shape, you will provide an exponential increase in value to your customers, and as a result, make more money.

cardio-vascular capacity. They would be more relaxed, and they would have higher self-esteem.

Now you tried to figure out: What were all the things that had to happen for a person to go from the out-of-shape condition to the in-shape condition? Obviously, they needed to work out at least three times a week for one hour. They needed to train with a coach to keep themselves going. They needed to have medical examinations as they went through the process. They needed yoga. They needed nutrition counseling. They also needed psychotherapy to unhook any mental or emotional blocks they had about fitness and health.

To facilitate the transformation, you linked these elements together in the right sequence. The first step was a vision and program planning session. The second step was a medical examination. The third step was a fitness session. The fourth step was nutrition planning. The fifth step was a yoga class. And so on.

As you tested and refined these elements and steps, you ultimately arrived at the perfect transformation process. You became confident that any person who went through the 18 steps of the program, and did everything they needed to do, would be totally transformed from out-of-shape to great shape.

By creating a process like *The Great Shape Formula*, you completely transformed your business. You went beyond the narrow perspective of your widget. You provided an exponential increase in value to your customers, and as a result, you made more money.

Your special program also raised the profile of your fitness club. Journalists did stories about how your new program worked. You gave speeches and went on television. You wrote a book and produced videos. Other fitness clubs called to ask if they could license your process to use at their club. Everyone wanted to know how this great process worked. Your BIG Idea became a star.

Transforming Our Economy

Many people acknowledge the industrial age economy has run its course. They just don't know what new economy should replace it. I contend this new economy will be *The Transformation Economy*.

Let's face it. The old economy—based on transactions—is obsolete because it doesn't work very well. It consumes vast amounts of energy, generates unsustainable levels of waste, and ultimately, it doesn't deliver *The Peak Benefit*. In fact, most industries in the industrial economy don't deliver very good results at all.

Think about the financial services industry. There are thousands of financial products and services. There are hundreds of financial institutions, and millions of financial advisors. There is a multitude of financial advice from TV shows, newsletters, and web sites. There are also thousands of courses and schools that teach people about money. But at the end of the day, how many people have their act together when it comes to their money? One percent? Two percent? At the most. So how can we say the financial services industry is working if it only delivers results for one or two percent of the population.

Why isn't it working? It's not working because the old economy is based on single, narrow-focused transactions. Each player in this economy—which I call *The Transaction Economy*—sell a specific product or service to their customer. In the financial services industry, one guy sells a mutual fund and walks away with his commission. Another guy does financial planning and walks away with his fee. But no one is helping his or her client achieve a total transformation. It doesn't even dawn on them.

The same is true in every other industry. Does the medical industry really work? Are people generally healthier? Do the pharmaceutical companies, and the hospitals really want people to get fit and live healthy lives? I'm not so sure. They would lose customers and patients.

Does the auto industry work? Do the car companies and the oil companies really want people to drive green-energy cars that don't need very much maintenance? Do they want society to transform its transportation systems for the better? I'm not so sure. They think they would lose customers.

Does the education system work? Are kids better educated these days? Are literacy and numeracy rates going up or down? Let's face facts; the education system is broken because no one sees the whole system as a transformation process. Like everything else in the industrial economy, education is delivered in a piece-meal fashion. Because it is based on a transaction model, the education industry is incomplete, chaotic and ultimately ineffective.

But imagine if the people in these industries adopted a transformation perspective. What if they developed a transformation process that helped their customers get in great shape? I am convinced it would transform our economy and allow us to tap into a well of endless new, big and exciting ideas. By changing their intentions—from doing a transaction to facilitating a transformation—all of these industries would grow well beyond their present-day size and influence.

I also believe this is a moral and ethical issue. Most people try to do good things in their work, but the transaction-based economy is inherently corrupting. It turns good people into salespeople who just try to sell something to make a buck or meet a quota. They convince themselves that it doesn't matter if their widget helps the customer as long as they sell it.

But this attitude is not sustainable. Eventually customers figure out that the widget doesn't help them achieve their *Peak Benefit*. That's why business people today are confronted with what I call *The Ethical Imperative*. It is imperative that they act ethically, or they won't achieve lasting success. In today's world—where word spreads quickly across the Internet and through other forms of instant communication—it's very difficult to achieve lasting success built on the wrong intentions. That's why I believe *The Transformation Economy* will work so much better. It will not only generate greater prosperity, it will also make business people feel better because they will be truly helping their customers.

That's my little sermon. But I truly believe it. If you have the right intentions, you can change your business to truly help people achieve a transformation. You will realize your widgets aren't the whole story, that there is so much more you can do. Then you will never run out of BIG Ideas to help people.

Chapter 8

The Three Cs:
Three Benefits Not Provided By Most Penguins

As we have learned, if you want to create a BIG Idea and stand out from the other penguins in your industry, you have to add more value than typically provided in *The Transaction Economy*. We've learned that you can develop BIG Ideas by helping your customers achieve their *Peak Benefit* and by providing a transformation, rather than a transaction. There is also a third way: By providing your customers with *The Three Cs*.

The Three Cs are *Caring*, *Coaching* and *Coordination*. These are three benefits rarely provided in the old transaction economy. Let's start with Caring. How many suppliers do you deal with that truly care about you? One or two if you are lucky. Then ask yourself: Do you truly care about helping your customers achieve their goals, or are you just trying to sell them something?

Consider Coaching. How many businesses take the time to coach their customers through a step-by-step process to make sure they have done everything they need to do to achieve their goals? Very few. Ask yourself: Do you coach your customers through a step-by-step process, or do you just complete a quick transaction? Are your clients missing some important steps because no one is coaching them through a comprehensive process?

Thirdly, think about Coordination. How many companies help their customers review and select all of the resources

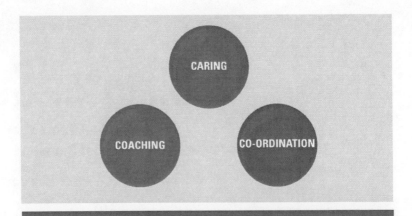

You can add more value—and make more money—if you provide your customers with The Three C's: Caring, Coaching & Co-ordination

available to them? Only a handful. Most companies just show their customers the small number of products and services they sell. They don't show their customers the whole picture. They leave that to the customers to do. So what about you? Do you limit your discussions to the resources you have to sell, or do you help your customers coordinate all the resources available in the economy?

Unfortunately, in *The Transaction Economy* there is very little Caring, Coaching, and Coordination. That's why your customers are so hungry for them. They are just waiting for someone to provide these benefits. That's your opportunity.

Begin with Caring. I speak to many business people who worry they are not providing enough value to their clients. This concern is commendable and heartfelt, but it's usually unfounded. If they truly care about their customers, they already provide 90% of the value they need to provide.

I say this because a lot of companies really don't care about their customers. They say they do, but their methods demonstrate the opposite. Because they focus on a transaction, and doggedly push specific products and services at their customers, it is clear they care first about themselves. It's sad, but true.

That's why people are so grateful when they meet someone who truly cares about them. It is such a rare commodity these days. So search your soul, and ask yourself: Do I truly care about my customers, or do I really just care about myself?

If you are honest with yourself, you might be surprised by your answer. Sure, you are a good person, but maybe the dog-eat-dog tenor of our competitive economy has sucked you into a dark place. If so, now is the time to reverse direction.

There are plenty of ways to truly care about your customers. The most important is to put their agenda ahead of your own. Your primary objective should be to help them achieve their goals. Make their success the source of your success. This sounds almost like a cliché, but it is rarely genuinely undertaken. Secondly, be willing to adjust and reshape your business to suit the needs of your customer. Stop being so rigid and dogmatic about your products and services. Thirdly, come up with new ways to help your customers by creating BIG Ideas. This will demonstrate that you care enough about your customers to always provide them with new valuable things.

Special Note: It's important to be Caring, but you also have to be careful about who you help. I am not talking about being a door mat. If people want to get your Caring, they are going to have to pay you well and treat you well in return. You can only care for so many people in your life so you have to be selective. That's why your BIG Idea isn't for everyone. It is only for people who appreciate how caring you actually are. Otherwise they don't deserve you.

Secondly, there is Coaching. In *The Transaction Economy*, there is usually only one step for the customer: Buy the product or service. The relationship is limited in scope. But there is so much more you can do. You can coach your customers through a step-by-step process that helps them completely transform their situation. You can have hundreds of steps, just like *The Great Shape Formula*.

Coaching is very valuable because you aren't imposing your will on your customers. You are empowering them. At each step, you're helping your customers think through their situation, and then make important choices. You aren't telling them what you do; you're helping them figure out what they need to do.

This approach is much different from traditional consulting. The consulting approach is to provide all the answers. You investigate the situation, and then you recommend that the customer do certain things. You try to sell them on your advice and recommendations.

In a coaching capacity you do something different. Instead of having all of the answers, you have great questions. You ask your customers: "What are your goals? What do you need to do to achieve those goals?" You don't have to have all of the answers; you just need to ask the right questions in the right order.

It is like you are a fitness coach. If you were a fitness *consultant*, you would do pushups for the client, and then they would complain they didn't get in shape. But a fitness coach gets the customer to do the pushups. Then the customer gets in great shape, and they thank you for it.

Coaching works better because your clients need to get important things done. But they don't know all of the things they need to do, or what order to do them in. They also need someone to help them along the way, and keep them accountable.

Acting as a coach, you can help your customers achieve incredible results.

Thirdly, we have Co-ordination. This is an extremely valuable role you can play for your customers. In today's time-stressed world, your customers are very busy. They don't have time to sort through all of the options they have. That's why many people prey on them to buy a single component of the puzzle. Feeling they need to do something, the customer buys the widget, but soon realizes that the transaction did not solve their problem. They also know there are many options out there, but they don't know which ones to choose, or how to pull them together in the most effective combination.

That's why people today need a Coordinator. They need someone who will show them all their options, not just the ones being sold by a transaction-based salesperson. They need a Coordinator to teach them about all of their options, and then help them select and use the best combination of them.

I will use my industry—the marketing industry—as an example. If you go to an ad agency for help with your marketing, what do you think they will recommend? Advertising of course. If you go to a direct mail company, they will recommend direct mail. And if you go to a web site design firm, they will recommend a web marketing campaign. Each player will only talk about their particular tool because that's how they make their money.

But our company does it differently. We act as a *Marketing Coordinator*. We help our clients develop a marketing plan and then we look at all of the marketing tools available. We look at advertising, direct mail, web sites, books, seminars, trade shows, hot air balloons, and many other marketing tools the client might need. We're objective because we're not attached to any particular tool. We just want to make sure our clients select the best tools for their plan. We then act as the Coordinator of the tools they need. For example, we might coordinate the marketing campaign of a client by working with an ad agency, a web design firm, and a direct mail company.

By providing Coordination services, you assume a much higher status in the mind of your customer. You are no longer a salesperson hawking a particular tool for your own self-interests. You are seen as an objective expert who has their best interests in mind.

This role of Coordinator also opens up huge opportunities for additional revenue. Your former competitors can become potential suppliers, and you can make money from the work they do for your clients. You no longer need to fear dealing with competitors because you know that you "own" the relationship with your clients.

Your clients will also appreciate your coordination service because it will save them time and effort. They will no longer have to shop around for different tools from different companies. They will understand their options better, and make more confident buying decisions. They will know they haven't missed anything important. They will also know they have a single source—you—to call whenever they need something. As a result, all future transactions done by the client will be done through you.

From a branding and packaging perspective, *The Three Cs* have a tremendous impact. By providing Caring, Coaching and Coordination, you no longer look like a penguin. You are a completely different animal. Your customers will see you as a unique person who is invaluable in their life. They will want to have a lifetime relationship with you.

The nice thing is: You will also provide more work for all those sad penguins out there. They will be perfectly happy to get work from your clients through you. The ironic thing is: By using *The Three Cs*, even the other penguins will see you as different and special.

So ask yourself: What can you do to provide more Caring, Coaching, and Coordination?

Chapter 9

The Value Pyramid:
Play A Bigger Role in The Economy

Now I know I've been quite sarcastic about penguins, and have probably ruffled a few feathers, but I still think they're cute. I just don't want to be a penguin. I want to stand out in a crowded marketplace.

That's why I say every penguin has an important role to play in our economy. Some will have a very high profile, and others will play a lesser role. Some of them will be highly acclaimed architects, while others will dig ditches. Both will be important, but it is the architect who will make most of the money.

As a penguin trying to break away from the pack, you have to decide what role you want to play. Do you want to be an architect or a ditch digger? I say it's a choice because it is. Your current role is not destiny, or carved in stone, it is just how you see yourself. Take for example, car salespeople. They decide what kinds of cars they sell. Some sell Rolls Royces and some sell Volkswagens. Fundamentally, they have the same skills and abilities; it's just that one of them decides to sell regular cars, and the other decides to sell premiums cars. That's why I say it's really how we see ourselves that matters. If we see ourselves selling Rolls Royces, that's what we do. If we see ourselves selling Volkswagens, that's what we do. Our destiny is really a personal choice; it's not imposed on us.

With this in mind, it is useful to realize there is a hierarchy of roles in every industry—which I call *The Value Pyramid*. Understanding this hierarchy will help you choose your most appropriate role and perhaps make a major leap forward in your business.

The Value Pyramid has five layers. Each layer represents one of the fundamental roles you can play in the economy: Theorist, Architect, Contractor, Builder, and Laborer. Let's review these from the top:

Theorist: A Theorist is someone who develops Models. These are models of what works and what doesn't. Frank Lloyd Wright created a new model of architecture called The Prairie School. Albert Einstein created a new model of the universe called The Theory of Relativity. In financial services, Harry Markowitz was one of the creators of Modern Portfolio Theory, used by millions of investment portfolio managers around the world. This is the highest role you can play in the economy.

Architect: An Architect creates Blueprints based on Models developed by Theorists. For example, an Architect might design a blueprint based on Wright's Prairie School model. Physicists developed a blueprint for laser technology based on Einstein's relativity model. And many portfolio "architects" use Markowitz's modern portfolio theory to develop asset allocation blueprints for their clients. The role of Architect is the second highest role you can play in the economy.

Contractor: A Contractor works on Projects based on Blueprints created by Architects. For example, a contractor helps build a house designed by an architect. He or she uses the blueprint as a guide to get all of the projects done. They also coordinate the activities of the people on the layer below them:

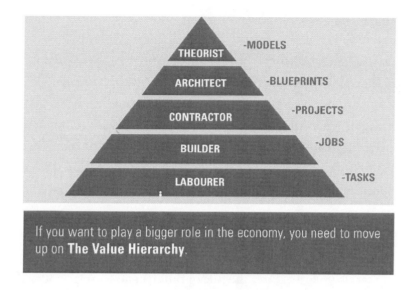

THEORIST -MODELS

ARCHITECT -BLUEPRINTS

CONTRACTOR -PROJECTS

BUILDER -JOBS

LABOURER -TASKS

If you want to play a bigger role in the economy, you need to move up on **The Value Hierarchy**.

the Builders. The contractor is third highest role you can play in the economy.

Builder: A Builder works on Jobs as a part of a Project coordinated by a Contractor. To stay with the construction analogy, builders are like plumbers, electricians, and carpenters. They have a specific skill set and perform a very narrowly-defined specialty. The builder is the role many penguins find themselves stuck in.

Laborer: A Laborer does Tasks as part of a Job managed by a Builder. They are the ditch diggers and day laborers who work on a job site. They do what they are told, and have very little knowledge of the overall scope of the work they are doing. This is lowest rung on *The Value Hierarchy.*

If you look at this pyramid closely, you realize every player in the economy finds themselves in one of these roles. As I said, each role is very important. They wouldn't have built the Hoover Dam without the ditch diggers. But the more important point is: Your role is not destiny, it is a choice. I believe most penguins can rise higher on *The Value Pyramid*. Most of them can, in fact, achieve the level of Theorist.

I say this because I believe all of us have theories we can package. All of us can create blueprints for our customers. And all of us can act as Contractors by coordinating projects. But that's not what most penguins do. They simply act as Builders. Stuck in *The Transaction Economy*, they simply provide their single, discreet service or product. As a result they make less money, have less status, and less power. They also look like all of the other penguins.

The Symbolspace Navigator

So how do you rise about the role of Builder and package yourself as an Architect and a Theorist? You begin by understanding how to navigate *Symbolspace*—a term I coined many years ago. I believe the new economy requires us to become adept at navigating the conceptual world (Symbolspace); to be good at developing and packaging models, concepts, and symbols. This is opposed to the old industrial economy, where wealth came primarily from manipulating the physical world.

Theorists are masters at conceiving and packaging concepts in *Symbolspace*. They take diverse ideas and concepts and pull them together into novel theories about how the world works. That's what Einstein did. He worked in *Symbolspace*. He didn't have to travel at the speed of light. He simply conducted thought experiments about it, and came up with a new model for how the universe works.

I believe we can all navigate *Symbolspace*. In fact, we are doing it all the time. We are always thinking about what works and what doesn't. When a little baby puts his hand on a hot oven window, he learns quickly what works and what doesn't. This helps him add a new element to his model about what works and what doesn't: Touching a hot oven is not a good idea.

By looking at your theories of what works and what doesn't, you can package yourself as a Theorist. Let's say you are a corporate recruiter. With ten years of experience, you know what works and what doesn't when it comes to recruiting new employees into a company. Your concept of what works becomes your Model. Your concept of what doesn't work becomes your Anti-Model. Presto. You are a Theorist. The key is to package these concepts and models with names like I do (i.e. *The Value Pyramid*, *The Transformation Economy*, and *Symbolspace*.)

The key point is: Every penguin has his theories, but only some penguins package them. And they are the penguins who write books, give speeches, and assume a high profile in their industry.

What about the role of Architect? Once again, every penguin can become an Architect. They just have to help their customers create a Blueprint by walking them through a step-by-step planning process. That's why I get all my clients to package a gourmet planning process: so they can assume the role of architect.

And thirdly, what about Contractor? You can also add value, and make more money, by packaging your services as a Contractor. You can help your customers achieve their goals by coordinating all of the Builders. Moreover, you will be the one to select the Builders, possibly some of your former penguin competitors.

Theorist, Architect and Contractor. These are three higher roles you can play in the economy, and as a result, increase your influence, profile, and income.

PART THREE:

Packaging Your Big Idea

Chapter 10

The Final Five Percent:
Why Packaging Is So Important

Are you just five percent more effort away from incredible success?

Back in 1962, there was a woman named Jean Nidetch who lived in Brooklyn. At that time, she weighed more than 300 pounds and wanted to slim down. So she went to a seminar at a local hospital and learned a few basic dieting tips. Very disciplined, she followed their advice rigorously and over six months she slimmed down to 130 pounds. This remarkable transformation stunned her friends and neighbors so much they asked her to help them lose weight too. So she started a little group in her home and charged her friends $5 a month.

Over the next three years, Jean helped hundreds of people lose weight, and she got a nice little business going. What she didn't know was: She was sitting on a goldmine. All she needed was the final 5%: packaging.

***

"To package or not to package?" that is the question. Is it nobler to remain unpackaged, or by packaging become something artificial and inauthentic? These are the questions many penguins ask themselves when they think of breaking away from the flock.

Packaging is often thought of in a negative light. We say politicians or aging rock stars are fake because they are "packaged." We say the vacuous actress is "all packaging." The notion is that packaging is used simply to pretty up something inconsequential or dishonest.

Certainly, packaging can be used to dress up something of little or no intrinsic value, but it is my contention that packaging is really meant to help others easily comprehend the real value and beauty of something. Done properly, it can help overcome misunderstandings, ignorance, and prejudice. It all depends on your intentions.

For example, I have met many business owners who are misunderstood. Their prospects think they are just like the other penguins. Their prospects can't see the special unique value they provide because their packaging doesn't communicate how they are different and better. They feel their business is the biggest secret in the world.

Many of my clients say that before packaging their BIG Idea, their prospects thought they were just salespeople trying to push a widget. They were perceived as quota-driven snake oil salespeople. Their prospects pre-judged them because their packaging didn't convey the true story; that they were caring people who just wanted to help.

Having completed the packaging process, it is now easier for my clients to quickly communicate their true nature and intentions. Any misconceptions are quickly dispelled. Their prospects get it immediately that they are not just penguins. Their new packaging helps them build trust faster, and develop lasting relationships with more great customers.

We have to remember that we are all "packaged." Everything we say, everything we do, and how we appear physically, creates a package. This package either communicates the right message or the wrong message. It either conveys a positive image or a negative image. In other words, even if you don't do anything, you are still packaged. But if don't package yourself with intention, your "unpackaged" packaging might not help you tell the story you want to tell.

The Difference Between Branding & Packaging

Many people throw around the words "branding" and "packaging" without giving you a clear definition of the terms. Some people think they are the same thing. Other people admit they really don't know what the words mean, but still express great interest in "branding" and "packaging" their business. Obviously, if we're going to use branding and packaging properly, we better start by defining the terms.

After considerable thought and debate I came up with the following definitions:

Branding: Your "brand" is the combination of feelings and thoughts about you and your company in the hearts and minds of your customers.

Packaging: Packaging is the combination of ideas, words, images, and experiences used to deliver your "brand" into your customers' hearts and minds.

In other words, your brand is something literally "inside" the hearts and minds of your customers, and packaging is what you do to get it there.

I like these definitions because they show how branding and packaging are different and yet linked together. You can't have one without the other. Your "brand" is a thing, a noun, and

Your brand is found in the hearts and minds of your customers.

Packaging is the combination of words, images and experiences used to deliver your brand into your customers' hearts and minds.

"packaging" is an action, a verb. Looked at from another angle, your "brand" is about your customers (how they think and feel), and "packaging" is about you and what you do.

Let's use Starbucks as an example. Their business, a combination of both tangible (coffee) and intangible (atmosphere) value, has a very strong brand in North America. When their customers think of Starbucks, they have strong, vivid thoughts and feelings. They think about great coffee prepared exactly the way they like it, a nice cozy sofa by a fire, and a friendly community atmosphere. These thoughts then evoke strong emotional responses fueled by the basic human needs for comfort, companionship, pampering, and status. The key point is: the value of Starbucks' brand is not something found in their stores, or their coffee, or at their head office. It is something found in the hearts and minds of their customers.

So how did Starbucks get their "brand" into the hearts and minds of their customers? They used packaging. They put together a "package" of ideas, words, images, and experiences that have made an indelible impression on their customers, and over time, the result has been a strong and positive "brand" in their customers' hearts and minds.

What makes a brand "strong"? The word "strong" when applied to a brand has two important connotations. First, if everyone in your marketplace knows your company, this is a sign that your brand is strong. However, being famous is not enough. Your brand is only truly strong if it evokes the right feelings and thoughts in the hearts and minds of your customers.

By "right" I mean two things. One, do your customers really understand what you do, how you are unique, and how you can really help them? Or do they have the wrong impression? Are they confused about what you really do? Do they erroneously lump you together with the penguins in your marketplace? And secondly, do they feel positively or negatively about your business? Do they love your company or hate it? Or are they simply indifferent? Obviously, only if your prospects clearly understand your business, and have positive feelings about it, is your brand truly "strong".

Why is a strong brand helpful? When your brand is strong, it makes it a lot easier to grow your business and take it to the next level. When your brand is well-known, you reach a larger number of prospects, and communicate your story with less effort. As well, if people already have a favorable impression of your company, they will be more open to your sales and marketing efforts, and trust you more. As a result, they will buy more with less resistance.

To further emphasize the power of a strong brand, think about what it would be like to have a "weak" brand. Imagine if your company was virtually unknown in your marketplace. Or imagine that most of your prospects had the wrong idea of what you do, or they had negative thoughts and feelings about your company. Under these circumstances, your marketing would obviously be less effective, and making sales would be more difficult.

I think we can all agree that having a strong brand is a good thing, if not a great thing. The next question is: How can you use packaging to build a strong brand for your company?

***

Branding and packaging are not inconsequential matters. I had one client Tom, a life insurance agent no one wanted to meet because they thought he was just a salesperson. They didn't know he was an incredibly caring person who had saved hundreds of families from financial disaster. But even after 25 years in the business, his packaging wasn't sending out the right message, and his branding was not what he wanted it to be. This made it harder for him to meet new people, and make more sales. After a quarter century, everyday still felt like an uphill battle.

I've worked with hundreds of companies in dozens of industries who have had the same lament. "No one gets what we do." "They think we're just like our competitors." "They think we're just trying to sell them something." "If only they would give us a chance, they would understand we are so much different."

The sad part is: Most companies provide incredible value and have a lot of unique things to offer, but their packaging isn't getting out the story. They have already done 95% of the work. They have amazing products and services. They have amazing customer service. But 95% is not enough. They need to add the other 5% (packaging) and that can make all the difference. In fact, doing that critical 5% more work on their packaging could generate thousand-fold returns on their investment.

***

Remember Jean Nidetch? She had a prosperous but small weight-loss business, but she didn't know she was sitting on a goldmine. She just needed to add that final 5%: Packaging.

One day, Jean met a professional packager. He said packaging would help her make more money and multiply the great work she was doing. He had a vision she could franchise her diet business, a concept not well known in those days. He said she just needed to document the steps of her transformative process, package it into a step-by-step system, and most importantly, give the whole thing a name.

Jean had never thought about naming her diet service. She could imagine naming a thing, like a car or a soft drink, but she never thought about naming an activity that was invisible and intangible.

But the packager convinced her a name would make a big difference. A name would make her story easier to tell. It would make her service more memorable. And most importantly, it would better convey the special ingredients of her diet system.

Jean asked: "Okay, so how do we come up with a name?" The packager said: "Well, what do you tell people to do in order to lose weight?" Jean said: "I get them to weigh themselves regularly. I get them to watch their weight."

The packager said: "That's it. Let's call it Weight Watchers."

After calling her diet system Weight Watchers, Jean packaged the step-by-step process she used to help her friends lose weight.

She packaged her diet system so other coaches could take people through the process. With this complete package in place, she was able to sell franchises around world, and in 1976 she sold her company to Heinz for a cool $360 million.

So, are you sitting on goldmine? If you do the final 5%—packaging—do you think you might be able to achieve exponential growth in your business?

Chapter 11

The Clock Is Ticking:
Creating A Theme For Your BIG Idea

I thought he was the most boring guy in the world.

I met him as an exhibitor at a financial services conference in California. He had come to our booth to take advantage of a free service we offered at the show called The Elevator Speech Packager. We promised to help attendees at the show upgrade their 30-minute info-commercial so it would be more interesting and effective. We also promised to do it in 15 minutes.

But this guy didn't give me much to work with. He was unbelievably boring. Everything he said about his business was generic and cliché. He was also very technical and went off on irrelevant tangents. After 12 minutes, I couldn't think of any interesting way to package his elevator speech. With three minutes to go, the clock was ticking.

***

The problem is: most penguins tell a boring story about their business. Their elevator speech is bland or too complicated, and it usually sounds like the speech of hundreds of other penguins. It is also inconsistent. Every time someone asks them what they do, the penguin scrambles to think of something clever to say, and then blurts out something clumsy or unsatisfying. That's because they've never worked on packaging their story—especially their elevator speech.

This is a big problem because you usually only have a short time to make an impression on a prospect. You have about 30 seconds to get your story across and it better be good. But if it is generic, such as "I am a lawyer" or "I am dentist", no one will ask any follow-up questions. Everyone already knows what lawyers and dentists do. People will simply file you under one of those categories and move on.

If your story is convoluted or complicated, you will confuse people. If you say, for example, you are "a spatial wealth engineer who realigns investment portfolios using Schopenhauer's kinetic centrifuge model," your prospects won't know what the heck you're talking about. They also won't bother to ask follow-up questions. They will just move on to someone else whom they can better understand.

In either case, if your story is generic or complicated, you won't connect with your prospect, and if you are boring or obtuse, you won't engage their interest. As a result, your prospect won't think you are different from the other penguins, and they won't go to the next step in the relationship. That will cost you business.

***

If you recall, I had three minutes remaining to come up with something good for the boring guy from Ohio. At that point, there was a crowd forming around the booth. People wanted to see me package elevator speeches. But I didn't have any ideas on how to make this guy more interesting.

Using a theme for your story—such as a lobster—will catch the attention of your prospects and help you stand out in a crowded marketplace.

But then I had an inspiration. I asked him: "Do you have any hobbies?" He said he did. He told me he collected clocks. He had more than 300 of them in his home back in Ohio.

I pictured a room filled with 300 clocks: grandfather clocks, alarm clocks, and cuckoo clocks. Lots of clocks all ticking away. So I said to him: "Why don't you say this: I help business owners realize their financial 'clock' is ticking, and I get them to make a plan before the alarm goes off."

There was a moment of silence, and then an eruption of applause. Everyone loved it. The guy from Ohio was thrilled. He now had an interesting elevator speech based on something he was passionate about. It was compelling and also begged follow-up questions. People would ask: "What does it mean that my financial clock is ticking? What will happen when the alarm goes off? What do you do to pre-empt these problems?"

The clock guy—formerly the boring guy from Ohio—now had a "hook" for his story. Clocks now served as an analogy or theme to make him more memorable. From now on, people would know him as the clock guy. In this simple but effective way, he would forever stand out from all of the other penguins.

The theme also gave him promotional ideas. When he got back to Ohio, he bought 500 inexpensive alarm clocks. He sent them out to prospects with the elevator speech written on a card. When he followed up, he said: "Did you get the alarm clock? Do you think your financial clock is ticking? Would you like me to help you before the alarm goes off?"

The approach worked because his theme stood out. Everyone remembered the clock. It also worked because it got people to think about their financial situation. It got them thinking that they needed to take action. As a result, he met a lot more prospects and made a lot more money.

***

So how do you come up with a hook for your story?

You can get your theme from anywhere. It might be a personal story. It might be an animal or an activity. It might be a movie you saw or a book you read. It might be a hobby.

I learned this lesson with my previous book *How To Sell A Lobster*. It is based on a personal story about how I won a waiter contest by selling 1,400 lobsters. (If you want to find out how I did it, I highly recommend you pick up a copy of the book).

It was my first book with a "theme". My other books were popular enough, but they were more like textbooks. There was no hook. They never fully captured the imagination of people.

But then I read the book *Who Moved My Cheese?* It is a cute book about little mice who have to deal with change. Hundreds of authors had written about change, but this book caught the imagination of people because the writer, Spencer Johnson, used an analogy. It didn't escape my notice that he sold millions of copies of the book.

So I decided to build my book around the theme of lobsters. I began the book with the lobster contest story, and then put a lobster on the cover. I wanted to make people wonder what the "lobster" thing was all about.

The strategy worked. *How To Sell A Lobster* has now been published in more than 25 countries in a dozen languages. I meet people all the time who say: "You're the lobster guy." I've become a minor celebrity in Japan where the book was a best seller. I get email from people in Japan who want advice from the lobster guy.

Using a theme works and it's also fun. I've learned that playfulness is next to godliness when it comes to making money. If you have fun with people, they will trust you and this will help you close more customers faster. We all think we need to be serious—after all, this is business for goodness sake—but I've found that fun sells better.

So I'm going to keep having fun. That's why this book is built around the theme of "penguins." I'm working my way through the animal kingdom. I'm thinking my next book will be about "elephants" or perhaps "raccoons."

Your theme can be straight-forward, as in the case of the clock guy, or it can be more mysterious, like the lobsters or penguins. I believe the mysterious themes work better because they create a dis-connect. For example, when people see a giant penguin at our trade show booth, they don't know what it means. It is dis-connected from their normal experience. When they see the penguin, and their brain experiences a dis-connect, they feel compelled to make the connection. That's why they come up to our booth and say: "What's this penguin thing all about?" And that's all I need. Now I have a chance to build a relationship with them.

A theme, either connected or dis-connected, must have a good underlying story that ties it all together. Otherwise, it is just something silly for the sake of being silly. That's why I tell the story about people in a particular industry who all look the same to their prospects, just like penguins. The whole idea of the theme is to reinforce some important point or lesson that you want your prospects to learn.

Here are examples of themes that have worked well for three of my clients:

The Groundhog Day Syndrome: Scott Ford is a financial advisor from Richmond Hill, Ontario. He was looking for a way to stand out from his competition, and get the attention of his prospects. He realized that a standard financial service ad in the local paper—with his picture, company name, and list of services—would get lost in a crowd of similar-looking ads. So we came up with a theme called *Overcoming The Groundhog Day Syndrome*.

"So what is *The Groundhog Day Syndrome*?" you might ask. Well, Scott says that most of his prospects are bored of their life, and have nothing to get excited about—especially during a downturn in the market. It's like they are living in the movie Groundhog Day where Bill Murray keeps living the same day over and over again.

It's a good story and really sums up the way most of his prospects feel. To communicate this mystery theme we created an ad with a picture of a groundhog, and we recorded a CD presentation. The groundhog theme is excellent because it gives Scott an interesting theme he can use for years for all of his marketing tools and activities.

The King's Armor: Dawn Frail is a speaker and coach who helps women become better leaders by using their female strengths. She created a program called *The Heart Method*. To promote this program, Dawn was looking for a theme that would get attention and also tell a meaningful story. She came up with *The King's Armor*.

Dawn says most women use male strengths when they are in a leadership position. But this doesn't work because they are trying to be someone they aren't. She says they have to use their female strengths: To lead from the heart.

To get this message across, Dawn told me the story of David and Goliath. When David was getting ready to take on the giant Goliath, the king lent him his armor. But the armor didn't fit very well, and David realized he wouldn't be able to use his real strengths while wearing it. So he took the armor off, and as we know, slew Goliath with a single stone from his slingshot.

Dawn says the same thing happens with women leaders. They try to put on a man's armor, and it doesn't fit. Encased in a male façade of strength, they fail as a leader. Dawn tells them to take off the male (king's) armor, and lead using their female strengths.

Dawn uses this theme in all of her promotional material. She has a keynote speech called *The King's Armor*, and has plans to write articles and a book by the same name.

Taming The Elephant: Patrick Carroll is a financial advisor. He is also the president of Wealth Strategies Group and the creator of *The Lifestyle Protector*. Recently, Patrick realized that the standard financial seminar—about investment and financial planning strategies—wasn't going to draw a crowd. He was looking for a theme that was new and different.

During several discussions with me, Patrick realized the true value he provides is helping his clients deal with their emotional relationship with money. He says people don't use their rational mind to make financial decisions; they usually use their emotions—sometimes to disastrous effect.

This reminded us of a book by Jonathan Haidt called *The Happiness Hypothesis*. Haidt says that people are like an elephant and a rider. The elephant represents a person's emotions, and the rider represents a person's rational mind. Haidt asks: If the elephant wants to go left and the rider wants to go right, which way will they go? Of course, they will go in the direction desired by the elephant. Haidt says most people follow their emotions and not the intellect; the elephant is in charge.

Because the story fit the subject matter, we decided to create a theme called *Taming The Elephant*: How to take charge of your emotional relationship to money. Patrick uses this theme for seminars and speeches to very positive reviews. People want to know what the elephant thing is all about. Patrick also recorded a CD with the same title and theme.

If you would like to create a theme to stand out from the other penguins, try these steps:

1. Determine the problem your prospects have and the lesson you want to teach them about how to solve it (i.e. business people all look the same and need to package a BIG Idea to stand out.)

2. See if you can come up with an analogy that parallels your message (i.e. It is just like a crowd of penguins that all look the same.)

3. Come up with a catchy title using the theme (i.e. The Problem With Penguins.)

4. Get an eye-grabbing picture that matches your theme (i.e. Picture of penguins at South Pole.)

5. Use the picture, title, and story in your marketing tools and activities (i.e. advertising, article, brochure, website, book, audio CD, and video.)

If you follow these steps, you will come up with a theme that will pull in prospects. Remember to have fun with it. Don't get too serious. People respond better when they are having a good time. Research also shows that rural, animal, and historical themes work best because they elicit a deep positive feeling in the prospect. Technological, urban, and sports themes don't work as well.

So the question is: What is your theme?

Chapter 12

Focusing The Mind:
Name Your Brand And They Will Come

Winston Churchill once quipped that nothing focuses the mind better than being shot at. Well that may be so, but naming is a much safer way to do it.

Giving a brand name to your BIG Idea is the best way to focus the mind of your prospect. You can tell them you develop and package marketing ideas, or you can tell them you have a program called *The BIG Idea Adventure*. You can tell them you do financial planning, or you can tell them you have a program called *The Wealth Success Solution*. You can tell them you are a dentist, or you can tell them you have *The Confident Smile Program*.

By using a brand name to describe something intangible, you make it more tangible. You transform something invisible into something visible. By christening your BIG Idea with a name you give it legitimacy and sticking power. In fact, scientists have confirmed that your brain is designed to store things with names. Without a name, your brain doesn't have anywhere to put the information it is receiving.

I discovered the power of brand names back in 1987, the year I started my business. I was working with a woman named Wendy. She had a commercial cleaning and pressing service.

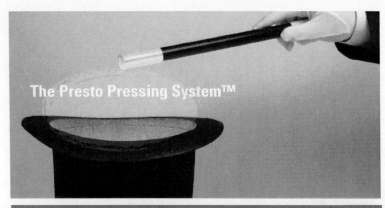

The Presto Pressing System™

Using a brand name for your BIG Idea—such as **The Presto Pressing System™**—will focus the attention of your prospects, and make your Big Idea easier to remember.

Clients sent Wendy their manufactured clothes to be cleaned and pressed before they were shipped to retail stores.

Wendy had a good business, but she had a problem. Because she was from Hong Kong, she struggled with her English. She was finding it difficult to explain her services quickly so prospects would work with her instead of a competitor.

During a few sessions, we came up with a brand name for her service. We called it *The Presto Pressing System*. We took everything she did and turned it into a "system." Then we added a benefit, the fact that it was (presto) fast and easy. The name also made it sound special: Not just your ordinary commercial cleaning and pressing service.

Using the name, Wendy had an easier and more compelling story to tell about her business. People responded by asking questions about her "system." She then walked them through the six steps of the process, which made it easier for prospects to see the full value of her services.

We also came up with a tag line: The Presto Pressing System: *We Know Your Needs Are Pressing.* It was fun and catchy, and also future-proof. She used the name and tagline for more than 20 years in all kinds of marketing campaigns. This packaging helped transform her business from a mom-and-pop operation into a major commercial enterprise.

Years ago, I worked with a fellow named Doug McPherson. He had a succession planning business in Maryland. Doug worked with construction company owners to help them sell their business or pass it on to the next generation.

Doug called me and said he had a problem. He said he could only meet his prospects early in the morning on a construction site. As busy people, they would only give him 15 minutes to explain his business. Doug said he couldn't do it. He needed at least an hour to really explain the full value of what he was offering.

Obviously, Doug needed to name his BIG Idea, and develop a better elevator speech.

During our discussions, Doug told me that construction companies always create a document called a Critical Path. This document sets out the step-by-step plan of how a building will be constructed, with deadlines attached to each step. He had been toying around with using this "critical path" theme for his BIG Idea. He wanted to call it *The McPherson Critical Path Process.* I thought it was a great idea and suggested he use it on his next sale call.

The next day, Doug went to a construction site. The owner told Doug he only had 15 minutes to hear what he had to say. Doug replied that he didn't need that much time. He said: "I have a program called *The Critical Path Process.* It will help you create a critical path for your succession plan." Astonishingly, the prospect said: "I need one of those critical paths. When can we get started?"

Doug quickly realized that the brand name for his BIG Idea helped focus the mind of his prospect. By using an analogy familiar to them, Doug didn't have to spend an hour explaining the whole thing. The prospect already understood the term "critical path" so he didn't need any more explaining. The prospect could also visualize the document he would receive because he worked with similar documents all the time. Acting as a shorthand device, the brand name enabled the prospect to make a quicker decision. It also allowed Doug to make a quicker sale.

Buoyed by his initial success, Doug used *The Critical Path Process* for years to significantly grow his business. He built a complete package around the brand name, including binders, booklets, and instruction manuals. Doug is now working on licensing his system and his packaged materials to other advisors. And it all started with naming his BIG Idea.

The Naming Process: Naming your BIG Idea might be easy. You might come up with a great name instantly. Sometimes, the right name is blindly obvious. In other cases, you might have to work at it for a while. In my case, when I have a BIG Idea, I try to come up with a "working" name as quickly as possible. I don't worry about whether it is a great name or not. It just gives me something to work with.

Coming up with a working name first takes the pressure off, and let's you start working on your idea. Often people get stuck because they try to come up with the perfect name. I worked with a woman who didn't like the working name we came up with. She wanted something better, and went away determined to figure it out. I didn't hear from her again, but a year later I ran into her at a conference. She said she didn't work on her BIG

Idea because she still hadn't come up with the right name. I told her she had wasted a year; that she could have been using her BIG Idea and making money with it, regardless of what name she used. I also told her she would have probably come up with a better name by actively using her BIG Idea. So learn from her mistake: don't get hung up on the name.

You also have to realize that you don't need to like the name you come up with. It just has to work. Years ago, I taught an Internet marketing workshop at a local university. It was a great course, but we only attracted 10 to 15 people. I started thinking maybe we weren't packaging it right. I was calling it *The Digital Marketing Workshop*. I liked the name because it conveyed that the subject was about more than just the Internet; it encompassed all aspects of the digital world. But it wasn't working. So I changed the name to *The E-Marketing Workshop*. I didn't like the name, because I thought it was too cliché and simplistic, but it worked much better. We signed up 50 people for the next workshop. So that lesson is important to remember. It's not whether you like the name, or whether your mother likes the name, it is about whether or not it works.

The Signature Activity: It is very effective if the brand name and elevator speech are built around a particular activity that is unique to you. I call this a *Signature Activity*. This tactic helps focus the mind of the prospect even more on what you are doing.

Doug McPherson communicated a *Signature Activity* with his brand name. His prospects could easily visualize working on a "critical path" document for their succession. This made it easier for Doug to explain his services, and for the prospects to buy them.

I use a *Signature Activity* in my brand name: *The BIG Idea Adventure*. I tell people I will help them develop and package a BIG Idea for their business. Specifically I tell them I will do it during a free 90-minute session called *The BIG Idea Outfitter*. This name works because most prospects are very interested in working on a "BIG Idea."

I have a client named Jason Greenlees. He developed a Signature Activity-based story for his program *The Total Financial Organizer*. He helps people totally organize their finances by pulling together a binder called *The Total Financial Organizer*.

Jason just tells them the story, and shows them a sample binder, and they say: "I need one of those. When can we get started?" It makes Jason's job so much easier, and helps him close more prospects faster.

Awkward At First: Be forewarned: It sometimes feels weird at first using a brand name for your BIG Idea. But you will discover that the name makes it easier to tell your story, and easier for your prospects to understand what you do. You just have to try it a few times.

A couple of tips about naming your BIG Idea:
- Keep the name to four or less words. You will get sick of saying a longer name.
- Always start with the word "The". The word "The" is what makes your intangible BIG Idea into a tangible thing.
- Don't use acronyms for your name such as TSSP or FGBY. You are trying to position your BIG Idea as a gourmet meal. Acronyms make it look like fast food.

- Search the Internet to check if anyone else is using the name. Try to register the domain name for it. If it is available, buy it.
- You can use the trademark symbol on your name. It indicates only that you are planning, someday, to register it with the government.
- Once you settle on a name, it's a good idea to have a lawyer register it with the government, as a "registered" trademark.

So what's it going to be? What's the name of your BIG Idea?

Chapter 13

The Concept Tornado:
Packaging Your Ideas and Concepts

I have a client who, before she worked with me, could only explain what she didn't do.

Mette Keating wasn't an interior decorator, wasn't a color specialist, and wasn't a feng shui expert. "Then what are you?" I asked her. "I don't know," she said. "I do all of those things, but not exclusively any of them. So to say I'm an interior decorator or a feng shui consultant isn't really true. I'm so much more than that."

Mette and millions of other people like her—consultants, advisors, speakers, authors, and other kinds of experts—are caught in the whirlwind of a problem I call *The Concept Tornado*. They have so many divergent ideas, concepts, symbols, and models swirling around in their head—like a tornado—that they can't explain what they do, only what they don't do.

The Concept Tornado is a huge problem in today's society because we are constantly inventing and re-inventing what we do. As we gather more information, knowledge and wisdom, from a wide variety of sources, we bring many different methods and modalities into our work. This convergence is very creative and helpful because it leads to new and more effective solutions to problems, but it also makes it harder to package ourselves. We can no longer use the old specialized labels—such as teacher,

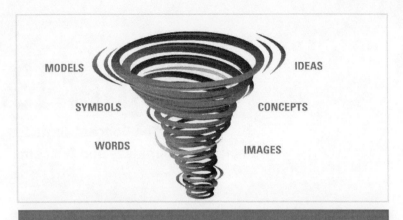

MODELS   IDEAS

SYMBOLS   CONCEPTS

WORDS   IMAGES

If you do many different things, **The Concept Tornado** makes it hard for you to explain clearly exactly what you do.

accountant, marketer, insurance advisor, and interior decorator—because those definitions only capture one element of what we do.

My wife Ginny had this issue. She is a physician who does psychotherapy (primarily on me, but that will be the subject of another book someday). She gives workshops for people who suffer from depression and anxiety. Her approach is very effective because she combines elements of Cognitive Behavioral Therapy, Gestalt Therapy, and Mindfulness Meditation, along with an eclectic mix of other influences, ideas, and methods. But for Ginny, although her workshops are very effective, at times they can be difficult to describe because she is combining three different modalities.

Gair Maxwell was another person twirling about in *The Concept Tornado*. His company, The Fundy Group, was helping clients build their brand by working closely with their employees. Gair and his team did great work, but they had a hard time explaining the theories and principles behind their approach. As

Gair told me: "We had a whole bunch of jumbled thoughts and half-baked ideas, but no single coherent theory. This made it hard for us to tell our story confidently and that cost us business."

Each of these three people—Mette, Ginny, and Gair—is typical of almost every thoughtful business person today. They have lots of great ideas and concepts, but they are not sure how to tell a simple story that pulls them all together. They also don't realize the way to escape *The Concept Tornado* had been staring them in the face for years.

***

So how do you escape from *The Concept Tornado*? It's quite simple. Stop thinking about you, and start thinking about your customers. Start thinking instead about the benefit your customers get from your convergent, cockamamie confluence of concepts. Then your single package will appear.

Let's start with Mette. I got her to think about her customers—business owners. I asked her: "What is the big problem your prospects have?" At first she said: "They have boring, uninspiring offices." I said that's fine, but what problems does that cause? "Well," she said, "It makes everyone in the office feel dead, and then they don't perform very well. They feel like they are working in The Dead Zone."

"So what *Peak Benefit* do you provide to solve this problem?" I asked. "I help them create an office where everyone feels truly alive," she responded. So then, I said: "Let's call your program *The Office Alive Solution*."

Mette loved the name and the concept because it pulled everything together. She no longer had to talk about interior decorating, colors and feng shui. She just talked about the client and making everyone feel totally alive in his or her office.

In Ginny's case, we focused on what skill she was helping her patients learn in order to ease their anxiety and depression. Ginny said the primary skill is to learn to become more mindful of their moods. This led to the name *The Mindful Mood Workshop*. With this title, she is better able to explain to her patients how all of the three modalities fit together in order to help them be more mindful of their moods.

Thirdly, there is Gair Maxwell. By looking at the situation from the perspective of the client, Gair said he helps them build a brand and then spread it seamlessly through the organization. He said: "Unless a brand is seamless, and all the employees are on board, it is unlikely the brand will be promoted consistently and effectively." Saying these words, Gair then said: "We should call our program *The Seamless Brand*."

Gair then took the concept of *The Seamless Brand* and now uses it for speeches and articles. He is also working on a book by the same name. Moreover, by defining and branding this single idea as his core package, Gair and his team now know the real benefit they are trying to help their clients achieve and this has made their work much more focused.

***

Sometimes it's okay to be in *The Concept Tornado*. You're just putting on lots of hats and accumulating the different conceptual elements of your personal theory. But you reach a point when you have to step up to the plate and package your own BIG Idea. The question is: Have you reached that point?

Chapter 14

Cosmic Taxi:
Packaging An Unexpected Experience

Most taxi drivers are penguins. They all drive the same kinds of cabs. They all drive you from A to B, and they all charge the same fares. Like penguins in other industries, you can't really tell one taxi driver from another. They are all the same.

But one night, I met a taxi driver who is decidedly not a penguin. My wife Ginny and I were going to New York, and we called a taxi to take us to the airport. When we got into the cab, we realized we weren't in Kansas anymore. The taxi was jammed from floor to ceiling with toys, trophies, flashing signs, action figures, and because it was Easter-time, a basket of Easter eggs. There was also a rack of magazines, and Bollywood music videos playing on a video screen. It wasn't what we were expecting, and at first we didn't know what to make of it. The taxi driver Akber welcomed us with an ear-to-ear grin, and explained: "It's all for fun. Just to brighten up your day. I call my cab *The Cosmic Taxi*."

As we drove to the airport, I realized that Akber was a man with a BIG Idea. He didn't want to be just another penguin in the taxi industry. He said: "People love riding in my cab. For them, it's a real experience. They've never been in any cab like it in their life."

My wife Ginny and I thought it was great. We laughed and joked with Akber all the way to the airport. He said people across the city call him specifically because they want to take his cab. "They call me because they want their friends and family to experience my cab. They also want to see what I will do next because I redecorate the taxi every season; for Easter, Halloween and Christmas."

Akber spends about $2,000 a season on stuff to put in his cab, but he says it's worth it. "I get 20 to 30% tips and I roll some of that back into decorating the cab."

Akber says other taxi drivers don't like what he is doing. "They think I'm crazy. They don't understand why I do all this and spend so much money on my cab. But I love it, and my customers love it so I don't care what they say."

Right on Akber.

I realized driving in his cab that Akber and his Cosmic Taxi embody the spirit of BIG Ideas I have been promoting for two decades. With a little imagination and a spirit of fun, Akber has reinvented the boring taxi industry. He gave us an experience that we will never forget, and we will tell everyone about. He isn't satisfied with just doing the same old thing, and now he makes tips that are two to three times larger than his other, less imaginative competition.

***

While packaging a BIG Idea often means selling a new product or service, the story of *The Cosmic Taxi* illustrates the value of also changing the customer experience; to start doing things differently. This means not just meeting or exceeding customer expectations, but doing something that your customers are not expecting.

The unexpected is what creates an experience. That's why traveling is so interesting and refreshing. When you live in a place for a long time, you get used to everything around you. You stop noticing the stores, the cars, and the people. You've seen everything so many times nothing stands out or catches your attention. Your mind goes into sleep mode.

But when you travel, you don't know what's going to happen next. Because you haven't been there before, your mind is hyper-alert. All kinds of new things happen, many of them unexpected. Assuming they are pleasant new things, it is an enjoyable and energizing experience.

That's what we want customers to feel; awake, curious and energized. When they are in that frame of mind, they are more likely to get interested in you and buy things from you. You can create this positive mood by doing things not done by the other penguins.

For example, most of the penguins in the financial services industry do exactly the same things. They ask their prospects to fill out a financial questionnaire. Then they meet with them and ask them some questions about their money. Then they put together an investment plan and present it to the prospect. If the prospect likes the plan, they become a client and give their money to the financial advisor.

That's the standard process, but it's boring because it's exactly what the prospect/client is expecting. They have probably done exactly the same thing with two or three other advisors.

But financial advisors don't need to be so boring. I know one advisor who has a limo pick up his clients to take them to a spa for a massage. Once they are feeling refreshed and relaxed, he meets with them to talk about their money. The clients love it because it's a different and fun experience. It's also one of the

With a little imagination, and a spirit for fun, you can create an unexpected experience your customers will never forget.

reasons they like working with him, instead of a boring penguin-style advisor.

There is a used car dealer who understands the importance of this concept. His name is Jim Gilbert, and he is Canada's "huggable" car dealer. When you go to his car dealership, Jim or one of his salesperson gives you a hug. It makes you feel welcome and special. His dealership also has teddy bears for the kids, and lots of other activities and special treats. It's unlike anything you've ever experienced before.

When Jim came up with this "huggable" idea, the penguins in the car industry laughed at him. They thought he had gone loony. But they were wrong. Jim's dealership—Wheels and Deals—in Fredericton, New Brunswick, is now the most successful used car dealership in Eastern Canada. He is a household name and has won several business awards. Everyone wants to visit his store and get a hug.

There is a phenomenally successful hamburger place near our cottage called Webbers that has packaged an "experience." When you get there, you start by joining a long line-up waiting outside. Instantly, you're greeted by an employee who has come outside to take your order. Within a short time, you enter the cooking area. The cooks are singing and dancing to loud rock music, and they look like they are having a great time. Their enthusiasm is infectious. You get excited. You start singing the songs. Within seconds, your order is ready, and you head out to a beautiful park to eat your burger and fries.

Going to Webbers is an integral part of the cottage experience for thousands of people. There is something about the process that gets under your skin. It's fun, it's fast, and the food is great. And the point is; the process itself is just as important as the food. Just going to Webbers is fun. That's why I tell people: "You've got to go to Webbers. It's an experience."

So what can you do to make your business more memorable by re-engineering the experience? How can you make it different? How can you make it more fun? How can you make it more memorable?

Chapter 15

The Two Restaurants:
Building Trust With Beautiful Design

Imagine an evening on the town. You and your date come across two restaurants, side-by-side, and you're thinking about which one to choose. You don't know it, but both restaurants have incredible food. Both chefs are amazing. The service is great at both places, and the prices are the same.

But there is one big difference between the two places. The one on the left looks a little seedy and rundown. The windows are dirty, and the interior looks dark and dreary. The décor is a mishmash of clashing colors. The other place is more beautiful. The exterior has a stunning mural flanked by two tall potted cedars. The menu is professionally designed with gold script and hand-drawn illustrations. Looking through the window, you can see that the interior design is spectacular. The tables, linen, lighting, artwork, and music create a warm and elegant ambiance.

Which restaurant would you choose? I'm guessing you would pick the second one. All other things being equal, most of us would pick the beautiful restaurant over the not-so-beautiful place. That makes sense, but why does it make sense?

From our research, we have concluded most people will choose the beautiful option because they trust it more. If they are trying to decide between two restaurants, as in our example, they will choose the beautiful establishment because logic says it will likely be cleaner, safer, more pleasant, and have more delicious food. On the other hand, they think that the ugly, ramshackle place will be dirtier, less safe, less pleasant, with inferior food.

No matter how we might want to kid ourselves, we all judge a book by its cover. It's a natural response. If we are in a hurry, and need to choose between two options, the safer bet is to choose the beautiful option. It might not always be the right decision, but it is the decision we will make 99 percent of the time.

In fact, research shows beautiful things actually do work better, simply because they are beautiful. In one study (described in detail in the book *Brands* by Marcel Denesi), a research firm built two ATM machines that were functionally identical. However, one had a beautiful interface (pleasing colors and graphics) and the other one was plain and drab looking. After observing people using both machines, it was found that users had a much easier time operating the beautiful ATM. They did their transactions faster and were less confused by its functionality. The researchers concluded the beautiful ATM worked better because its aesthetic appeal made the users feel more comfortable and confident about using it. In other words, its intrinsic beauty made people feel better, which in turn, helped them to think better.

That's why physical packaging is so important. If your physical packaging (such as logos, word marks, stationery, brochures, websites, and office space) is not beautiful, people may not trust you, and it will be harder to get them to buy your BIG Idea.

In his book *A Whole New Mind*, author Daniel Pink stresses this point: "For business, it's no longer enough to create a product that's reasonably priced and adequately functional. It must be beautiful, unique, and meaningful, abiding what author Virginia Postrel calls 'the aesthetic imperative'." Pink goes on to explain that beauty has now become an important point of differentiation in any environment populated by a large number of competitors selling what is essentially the same thing. As a result, companies today are making greater investments in physical packaging.

So how do you create physical packaging that is beautiful and meaningful to your prospects? It is all about planning and integration.

Planning and Integration: We use a tool we created called *The Design Map* to help us plan and integrate all of the physical packaging our clients need—both immediately, and in the future. These packages include logos, word marks, business cards, stationery, brochures, websites, books, binders, and hundreds of other possibilities. Once we have selected the elements, our design team develops the graphic design for each element so we can see what they will look like when fully completed. This map gives us a clear vision of the future, and makes sure all of the graphic elements are integrated.

By using *The Design Map* first, before you produce and print anything, you can test the impact of your intended design scheme on prospects, clients, and focus groups. The testing reveals if the look you've chosen is meaningful and appealing to your intended audience. If not, you then have the ability to change it to a more effective look.

We use *The Design Map* to help our clients avoid *The Fragmented Design Trap*. This problem happens when you design your materials one piece at a time over several months or years. During that time, you may change your designers, or your tastes, and as a result, you may end up with a patchwork of different looks, colors and images that don't fit together and project an unprofessional image.

All other things being equal, people will buy the more beautiful option because they trust it more.

Evocative Design: It is also important that your physical packaging evokes the desired feelings in your prospects. That's why the images, colors, and overall layout of your physical packaging need to be consistent with, and supportive of, the messages conveyed by your theme and story. For example, for the overall look of our business we use the color green and images from nature. We use this "design aesthetic" because we want to evoke the ideas of growth and adventure.

Determining the right look for your physical packaging is not an exact science, but you can test different looks on your prospects to see which work best. Try different colors, images, and layout styles, to see which combination evokes the desired feelings. Once established, this "style guide" will make your business more visible, meaningful, and memorable.

The Importance of Trust: Unfortunately, many business owners dismiss or neglect design at their peril. They think: "As long as we do a good job, it doesn't matter what we look like. People can see through all that fancy design stuff." But this assumption is wrong. If you are trying to sell your BIG Idea, building trust is incredibly important. Because your prospects can't see what you're selling, they are looking for ways to determine if they can trust what you are telling them. And if your physical packaging is amateurish, unattractive, or fragmented, they will have a hard time believing your BIG Idea is as great as you say it is. It will then be harder to get prospects to commit, which will cost you time, money, and effort.

Another important point to consider is this: While conceptual packaging affects your customers on a rational level, physical packaging affects them on an emotional level. Your customers will either get a good feeling or a bad feeling about the physical images you present to them. They may not be able to express their feelings in words, but they will put them into action. If they see something they consider beautiful, they may buy it. If they don't feel it's beautiful, they probably won't.

That's why it's important for you to make the investment in physical packaging by working with design professionals. It is not an option; it is critical to the success of your company.

Chapter 16

The Stay-Puft Marshmallow Man:
Packaging An Icon You Can't Get Out of Your Head

At the climax of the movie Ghostbusters, the Sumerian god Gozer arrives at the top of an apartment in Central Park West (New York) and tells the Ghostbusters that the next thing they think of will be the form he will assume to destroy the world. The Ghostbusters try to completely clear their minds, but Ray, played by Dan Akroyd, can't stop himself from thinking of something from his childhood: The Stay-Puft Marshmallow Man. Then seconds later, a giant version of the character is seen walking towards the apartment building with malevolent intent.

I love that scene because it illustrates how marketing icons and characters can stick in our head forever. Icons like Mr. Clean, the Goodyear Blimp, the Eveready Bunny, and Prudential's Rock of Gibralter. These characters or images represent the company in our mind and we never forget them. These icons become part of our cultural landscape, part of the *Symbolspace* I talked about earlier in the book.

To help you stand out from the other penguins, I suggest you create a character or image that represents your business and its BIG Idea. I call this your *BIG Icon*. This notion builds on the theme approach discussed in chapter 11, but now we are focusing on design and physical packaging.

I've got a few characters and icons I use to great effect. My previous book *How To Sell A Lobster*, made "lobsters" one of my *BIG Icons*. The book has a lobster on the cover, and I take lobster plush toys to speeches and trade shows. I've become known as the "lobster" guy. No one ever forgets it. In the book I also created a character named Marketing Mike. Everyone is fascinated about "who is Marketing Mike?" He is also the face on the cover of our BIG Bucks, the promotional money we give out at our workshops.

For this book, I'm using "penguins" as my *BIG Icon*. Everyone loves penguins and now when they see one they might also think of my company and me. In many ways, we've taken ownership of the "penguin" in our marketplace. (Someone asked me: Did you ask the penguins if it was okay to use them as your *BIG Icon*? The answer is no because I wasn't sure who to contact.)

We have clients who use all kinds of images to focus the minds of their prospects, and make their company more memorable. Pat Carroll uses elephants. Scott Ford uses groundhogs. Dawn Frail uses a women in a suite of armor. They use these icons because now people have another way to remember them.

Almost anything can work. You can use animals, geographic images, historic characters, types of buildings (i.e. lighthouses), and even make a play on your name. There is a condo real estate broker in my city named Brad Lamb. He runs billboards showing his head on the body of a lamb. It is a little perverse, but you never forget his name: Brad Lamb. There is another real estate broker named Wall, who uses a brick wall as his *BIG Icon*, and another one named Cherry who uses the fruit as her image.

I work with a real estate developer in Phoenix, Ricky Lyons, who uses the Inukshuk as his *BIG Icon*. An Inukshuk is a giant stone sculpture that Inuits in the north use as guideposts. Ricky uses this image to communicate that his company is stable, enduring, and provides direction to its clients. In his marketplace, the Inukshuk is synonymous with Ricky's company, Champion Partners.

To come up with your *BIG Icon*, you need to be creative, but not just for its own sake. The icon needs to have a story behind it. Earlier in the book I mentioned the guy from Ohio who uses clocks as his *BIG Icon*. It works because the image is also linked to his story about how "your financial clock is ticking." He is able to draw a connection between the clock and why it is relevant to the prospect or customer.

The great thing about a *BIG Icon* is that it has "legs." You can use it forever. KFC has been using Colonel Sanders as its icon for forty years. McDonalds has been using Ronald McDonald for just as long. Then there is the Goodyear Blimp. I can't imagine they will ever give up that icon.

Longevity is a primary principle of a *BIG Icon*. The longer you use it, the more powerful it becomes. Every time your customers see the image, they associate it with you, and that imprints your brand even more deeply into their mind.

Your BIG Icon can also be embedded in your logo and marketing material. Our logo is comprised of a lower-case "b" with a seed in the middle of it. We also use the image of a mature walnut tree on our brochures. If someone asks about these images, we say: "Our clients come to us with the 'seed' of a BIG Idea, and we help them grow it into a large, healthy, and successful 'tree'." This works well because it makes sense and it quickly explains how we can help them.

It's important to select your *BIG Icon* carefully. You don't want to use an icon already employed by another company, even if they're not in your industry. It will confuse people and

Using a penguin as my Big Icon helps prospects remember me and my story.

you might get sued. Also be careful that your *BIG Icon* is not too obscure. Using the image of an obscure person, character or event, might seem clever to you, but other people might not make the connection. It's also good to avoid anything too cliché, like sports or military images. They've been used a million times, and have lost their impact.

Using a *BIG Icon* is a strategy that works, but very few people ever do it. Maybe they don't know what icon to use, or they have never thought of doing it. But now you have no excuse. So what's your BIG Icon?

***

Hopefully, this section has given you guidance on how to package your BIG Idea so it will truly stand out and attract the kinds of prospects you want. Now we turn to the next section about how to sell your BIG Idea.

PART FOUR:

Selling Your Big Idea

Chapter 17

The Magnetic Marketer:
Why You Need To Stop Knocking On Doors

Imagine this scenario. There's a guy knocking on the door of your office. "Hi. I'm Karl from across the street. I'm a lawyer. If you need any legal help, give me a call. Here's my business card."

Afterwards, holding the business card in your hand, you think: "Who is this joker? He can't be a very good lawyer if he has to go around knocking on doors." Disdainfully, you toss his card into the garbage bin, and never give Karl another thought.

Silly right? I mean, you're not going to hire a lawyer who comes knocking at your door. If he does that, he can't be a very good lawyer. If you need a lawyer, you will find a great lawyer, someone who is successful, someone who is in great demand. Not some loser who comes knocking on your door.

When you think about it that way, it's obvious that knocking on doors gives people the wrong impression. It makes you look like a salesperson, someone selling something. It doesn't make you look like a successful, in-demand expert. It makes you look like a vacuum cleaner salesperson. And yet, that's what most business owners and professionals do. To get business, they knock on doors.

Keep in mind, I'm using "knocking on doors" as a metaphor for many kinds of overt, dynamic selling including cold telephone calls, direct mail, e-mail broadcasting, soliciting referrals, and advertising. It also includes literally knocking on doors.

These techniques don't work anymore for a number of reasons. First, as we've discussed, your prospects are hiding behind a sales pitch bunker. They are sick and tired of salespeople knocking on their door, so they don't respond. Second, knocking on doors gives your prospects the wrong impression. Just like the lawyer, if you knock on doors, your prospects will think you are desperate. And if they think you're desperate, they will conclude you aren't very good at what you do.

Most importantly, knocking on doors makes you look like a salesperson who's trying to sell a product or service; like magazine subscriptions or reusable diaper services. But that's not who you really are. You're an expert. You have a tremendous amount of knowledge, expertise and experience to offer. That's what you're really selling. But if you knock on doors, they won't see that. They'll just see "salesperson." And that will stop you from meeting lots of great prospects.

It's important to realize that these two roles "salesperson" and "expert" do not go together. They are not compatible brands. You are either one or the other. If you act like a "salesperson", your prospects will never be able to see you as an "expert".

That's why you need to market yourself in a totally different way. Instead of knocking on doors, you need to get people to knock on your door. Instead of being a Sales "Pitcher" you need to be a "Magnetic" Marketer. You need to stop using traditional sales techniques, and start using "magnetic" marketing techniques.

The Magnetic Marketing Model

I've taught hundreds of business owners—such as financial advisors, consultants, lawyers, accountants, architects, health care

Sales vs Marketing: Salespeople knock on doors, magnetic marketers get people to knock on their door, or call them.

practitioners, and even manufacturers, retailers, and restaurant owners—how to get prospects to knock on their door. I've taught them simple, but unconventional techniques that draw people to them, and reinforce their image as an expert. They report back to me that these techniques are easier, faster and less expensive than selling. And most importantly, they tell me that they work better.

To understand how Magnetic Marketing works, it is necessary to make a comparison between a Sales "Pitcher" and a "Magnetic" Marketer.

The Sales "Pitcher" knocks on doors.   They are product/service focused, direct, and appeal to the rational mind.   They don't achieve high sales because they don't break through the Sales Pitch Bunker.

The "Magnetic" Marketer gets people to knock on his or her door. They are value-focused, indirect, and engage the prospect's emotions. They achieve higher sales because they get prospects to come out of their bunker.

Magnetic Marketers have learned six skills that evoke strong emotional responses. They:

1. Create a Mystery (Curiosity)

2. Package and offer something New, Better, and Different (Excitement)

3. Foster a sense of Popularity (Trust) and Scarcity (Fear)

4. Give away Free Value (Desire)

5. Offer Choices (Empowerment)

6. They insist on a Yes or No (Urgency)

7. And they do a seventh thing, but I'll tell you that bonus one at the end.

In the next chapters, we explore each of these techniques in detail.

Chapter 18

Creating A Mystery:
Make Your Prospects Curious About You

"They don't know what to make of the penguins."

That's what I realized at a convention in Atlanta. I had a booth at the show, and I was using Mystery Marketing as a strategy. My booth had a banner showing a giant penguin with the caption: Have you got *The Penguin Problem*?

When people walked by the booth, they looked at the penguin picture, and they didn't know what to make of it. That made them curious. Then they approached me and asked, "What's *The Penguin Problem*?" That gave me the opportunity to tell my story about how most financial advisors look exactly the same in the marketplace—just like a crowd of penguins—and why they need to package their BIG Idea to stand out in their marketplace.

This strategy worked great because it drew people into my booth. They weren't expecting to see a giant penguin at a financial service trade show, so it caught their eye. The mystery also made them curious. They had to find out what this penguin thing was all about. They wanted to know the story.

This mystery marketing strategy also worked because my prospects now had the penguin "hook" implanted in their brain. After the show, I called them and said: "Remember me? I'm the penguin guy." And they replied, "Oh yeah, the penguin guy. I remember you." And most importantly, they also remembered

When you create a mystery, your prospects will become curious and approach you; they will then knock on your door.

the story, and why they needed to package their BIG Idea: To solve *The Penguin Problem*.

This mystery marketing theme—built around penguins—has also been scaleable: I've used the penguin hook for an audio CD, a webinar, an article, a speech, and for this book.

Why Most Promotions Don't Work: I've learned that most promotions don't work because:

1. **There is no dis-connect:** Communications experts may have taught you how to connect with your audience by speaking clearly and making eye contact. That's important. But you have to start with a dis-connect, otherwise you don't get their attention. If your message is too straight-forward, you don't stand out and catch your prospect's attention. Your sign, ad, or poster just blends into the surroundings. But when people are confronted with something dis-connected—like a giant penguin at a

financial trade show—their brain tries to connect these two disparate concepts together.

2. **There is no mystery:** Most people clearly state exactly what they want to communicate such as: "We are a computer company. We manufacture the best computers. Our computers have all kinds of great features." This message is very nice and helpful, but it doesn't leave anything to the imagination. There is nothing to be curious about. The person absorbs this information and then moves on to the next thing. But if you set up a mystery—Do you have *The Penguin Problem*?—the person gets curious and wants to solve the mystery. They approach you and say: What is this all about? Why do you have (a giant penguin) at a financial service trade show? This brings them deeper into your world.

3. **There is no underlying story:** Most people explain features and benefits. They don't tell a story. It is just a recitation of facts and figures. As result, the promotion doesn't make a lasting impression on the prospect. It is in one ear and out the other. On the other hand, if the promotion communicates an interesting story—with a beginning, middle and end, plus a lesson or moral—you make a lasting impression on your prospect. They remember you, they remember your story, and they learn the lesson you are trying to teach them.

4. **There is no call to action:** Most promotions do not make a connection between the story and the next step. There is no "call to action". As a result, the prospect takes in the information but doesn't know what to do with it.

This makes the whole promotion ineffective—after all, the point is to get prospects—and often makes it a total waste of time and money. That's why it's important to clearly state the next step: In our case, it's a free 90-minute starter session called *The BIG Idea Outfitter*.

That's why you should come up with a Mystery Marketing Idea: It works better. It just requires some creativity and time to develop a marketing strategy. It also takes the courage to stand out by doing something unusual, something a lot of people are afraid to do.

Chapter 19

Something New:
Get Your Prospects Excited About You

If you learn one thing about marketing from this book, learn the concept of "new". If you want to make more money and grow your business, you need to constantly come up with new things to tell your prospects and customers. You need to become a marketer of the "new."

Most marketing efforts fail because the underlying concept is old, generic, or not significantly different from other products or services on the market. You can have the most amazing website, and the most beautiful brochure, but if the basic idea and message isn't new, you won't get a lot of attention, and you won't excite your prospects.

That's why I developed my coaching program around the concept of the BIG Idea. Every marketing strategy must begin with a critique of the central idea: Is it new? Is it better? Is it different? Is it a BIG Idea? If not, then you have to come up with a BIG idea. Otherwise, you could waste a lot of time, money, and effort.

You also have to keep in mind that BIG Ideas eventually turn into Old Ideas. I remember when the idea of "financial planning" was a BIG Idea. That was back in 1985. People were really excited about this new concept. But that was more than 20 years. Today, financial planning is an old concept. No one gets excited about it anymore. It is still useful, but it's not exciting. The same goes for fax machines, e-mail, diet programs, mutual funds, all-inclusive resorts, ATMs, and "do-it-yourself" anything. In their day, these things were really BIG Ideas, now they are old ideas that don't get people excited.

So like it or not, you have to keep reinventing yourself. It sounds like a lot of work, but in fact, it's what your soul is telling you to do. You may think you want to have a single, permanent idea to sell forever, but that would be boring. It also wouldn't help you grow as a person. That's why I believe it's important for your mental health to keep coming up with new BIG Ideas for your business. It keeps your customers happy, and it keeps you happy. It also acts as a magnet to attract more prospects.

Here are few examples of what I'm talking about.

The Open Being Method: Jay Miller is a successful voice coach. He has worked with hundreds of business people, actors, and speakers. When I met Jay, he was very successful, but he also wanted to do more with his business. He felt there was more he could offer his clients. He was also concerned about the fact that there were many other people promoting themselves as "voice coaches."

After analyzing his business, the needs of his customers, and discussing Jay's aspirations as a professional, we came up with a higher level *Peak Benefit*: helping his clients with more than just their voice—helping them become more open as a person in three ways— Open Voice, Open Body, and Open Mind. This gourmet concept, which we packaged as *The Open Being Method*, is really exciting for Jay because it is new, better, and different.

It also gets the attention of his prospects because they've never heard anything like it before.

The Open Being Method is also great for Jay because it gives him plenty to think about. As a new concept, Jay can think about how to best open up people's voices, bodies, and minds. This intellectual journey will keep his mind alive, creative, and engaged for years to come, and this personal excitement will get his prospects and clients excited as well. And that's an important point. Typically, your old ideas have run their course intellectually. You already know 99% of the subject. Sure, there is always more to learn, but that extra 1% isn't going to get you jazzed up. But a new BIG Idea, with lots of new avenues of creative and intellectual exploration, will keep your mind sharp and alive.

The Level Three Program: Jean-Luc Lavergne is the president and founder of Lavergne Industries. His company provides molders and original equipment manufacturers (OEMs) with resins and compounds for manufacturing plastic products like printer cartridges. The resins and compounds are created from recycled materials. When we first spoke with Jean-Luc, he was looking for a BIG Idea to stand out from the competition, and get his prospects more excited. He also wanted to raise the status of his company in the eyes of his customers—from sellers of resins to purveyors of expert advice and service.

Together with his team, we came up with a BIG Idea called *The Level Three Program*. It is a consulting and accreditation process that helps OEMs develop more environmentally-friendly manufacturer processes. As clients work through the process, they are certified at level one, level two, and then level three. They can then use this accreditation, similar to ISO 9000, as part of their marketing.

Your prospects will only get ecxited if you tell them about something new, better and different: a Big Idea.

Jean-Luc and his salespeople are excited about this concept because it is new, better, and different. His competitors are talking about resins, while Jean-Luc is talking about a complete transformation. It doesn't mean that Jean-Luc isn't trying to sell his resins, he just realizes that resins are an old idea: *The Level Three Program* is a new BIG Idea that attracts prospects to his company.

Don't Kill Your Partner: Rick Bauman has been working as a coach for more than 20 years, primarily with insurance brokers and their teams. Rick was looking for a new BIG Idea that would take everything to a higher level, and position his company as unique in the marketplace. He came up a program called *Don't Kill Your Partner*.

Rick says many business partnerships are dysfunctional. The partners don't share the same vision, they are not working in the right roles, and they don't communicate with each other in a meaningful way. As a result, their organizations flounder because the partners feel like "killing" each other.

To overcome these issues, Rick created a program that helps business partners work out their issues by having meaningful conversations facilitated by one of his coaches. This helps them develop a shared vision, assume the right roles, and build a unified team.

Rick is really excited about this BIG Idea because there is nothing like it in the marketplace. It incorporates Rick's many years of experience, and gives him something exciting to work on. It also attracts the attention of many business people who don't really want to kill their partner.

As you can see, having new BIG Ideas is great for everyone. It gets you excited again about your business. It gets the attention of prospects. And it gives you something new, and more lucrative, to sell. It also differentiates you from the pathetic penguins in your industry.

So stop clinging to your old idea, and come up with a new BIG Idea.

Chapter 20

Popularity and Scarcity:
Make Your Prospects Feel Safe and Afraid

There are two things people want more than anything else: One: What everyone else wants (Popularity); and Two: What they are afraid they might not be able to get (Scarcity).

People gravitate towards something popular for the simple fact that it's popular. They don't want to miss out. They don't want to be left out. They want to be part of the in-group. It makes them feel safe.

Secondly, people also want something they fear they might not be able to get. If it looks like something might run out, they feel fear and they grab it, even if they aren't sure they really want it. It's just safer to grab it and work out the details later.

If you want to be a successful marketer, you must get your mind around these two concepts: popularity and scarcity. You need to make your prospects and customers feel both safe and afraid at the same time.

In my book *How To Sell A Lobster*, I told the story about *The Line-Up*. In order to get a new restaurant started, we made it appear to be both popular and scarce. We filled the place by giving away free food and drinks (popularity) and then we created a line-up out front (scarcity). True to form, people started lining up because it made them feel safe to be part of something popular, and yet also fearful they might not be able to get in.

This sounds manipulative because it is. But I don't feel bad about it. My client needed to do something or he would have gone out of business. We needed to prime the pump, so we fostered a sense of popularity and scarcity. And if you don't want to go out of business, you might need to do the same thing.

These techniques also engender secondary feelings of trust and urgency in the mind of the prospect. If something appears popular, then they will trust it more. After all, if it is popular, then it must be good. Secondly, if something looks scarce and in danger of running out, then the prospect realizes there is an urgent need to make a decision.

Safety and fear go together hand in hand. As human beings, we are more wired towards safety and fear rather than towards risk and opportunity. This safety/fear instinct probably has its origins in our heritage as hunters and gatherers. Back then, if we wanted to survive, it was wise to keep our eyes and ears attuned to danger, and to seek safety above all else. Taking risks to capture an extra-large buffalo usually ended in tears rather than triumph.

So most of us are wired for safety and fear. That means it is safer to choose something popular, and it is better to grab something that we fear might soon run out.

For these reasons, you have to make your BIG Idea appear both popular and scarce right out of the gate. Your prospects have to see lots of people using your BIG Idea, and they have to get the sense there is a limited supply that might run out.

That's why I gave my BIG Idea Adventure program away for free to 20 clients when I first started out. I wanted to create an impression that my program was very popular; that I already had lots of members who loved the program. This aura of popularity worked, and since that time, we have had hundreds of people go

If you create a line-up, you will foster an aura of popularity and scarcity. This makes your customers feel both safe and afraid at the same time.

through the program. But the program might have died an early death if I hadn't primed the pump first.

I'm also very careful to create a sense of scarcity around my time. I only have a limited number of time slots when I am available for coaching. I also don't take calls from clients and prospects directly. They have to make an appointment to speak with me. By limiting access, I create a sense of scarcity, and therefore, people want to meet with me even more.

That's why I'm not so crazy about the 24/7 service policies some business owners promise. They say: "You can call us 24/7. We will take your call anytime and anywhere. Well, I don't know about you, but that's not the kind of life I want to live. But most importantly, 24/7 access may make you appear too readily available, and as a result, your clients may not fully value or respect your time. (Granted, some businesses need to provide 24/7 service. But many other companies do it to the detriment of their image.)

***

So make sure you do these two things. Create an impression of popularity for your product or service. Give it away free to a few customers so others can see it being used. Secondly, don't make yourself, or your product/service, too readily available. Limit access. Make your customers wonder if they can get an appointment with you. Make them wonder if your products and service might be in scarce supply. If you do, they will want you or it even more.

Popularity and Scarcity. Safety and Fear. Trust and Urgency. These emotional triggers are the stock in trade of all Magnetic Marketers.

Chapter 21

The Free Value Strategy:
Make Prospects Come Out Of Their Bunker

Imagine your BIG Idea is a box of chocolate.

As a Sales "Pitcher", you hold up the box and tell prospects all about the great chocolates inside. They are delicious dark chocolates from Belgium. You bring out people who have eaten the chocolates: "These chocolates are great," they say. Using this approach, you make a few sales, but it takes you a lot of effort and a lot of time.

As a 'Magnetic" Marketer, you do something different. You simply give them a piece of chocolate from the box. A huge crowd forms. Everyone wants a free piece of chocolate, and when they taste it, they want to buy the box. It's that simple.

That's why I recommend you give away part of your BIG Idea for free. Not the whole thing, just part of it. Instead of talking about it, just give them a free sample. Demonstrate how great your BIG Idea is. Let them experience it first hand. This will evoke a strong feeling of desire in your prospects.

Some people have a hard time with this concept. They bristle at giving away something for free. "That will cost too much money," they say, forgetting how much they spend on sales techniques that don't work. "People will take advantage of my generosity," they say, forgetting that their generosity will attract a hundred times more prospects.

If you give away free value—such as a piece of chocolate from your box—your customers will desire it and come out of their bunker.

The great thing is: The free value you give away is something you already do or make. You already make chocolates. Just make a few more and give them away. You already have lots of ideas and strategies. Just give a few of them away for free. Then they will desire it more.

I met a guy recently who said he would never give away anything for free. He said he would only give clients his ideas and advice after they hire him. But I never found out whether his ideas and advice were any good, because he never gave me any. As a result, I never bought what he was selling. I didn't have any desire to.

Parsimonious. Stingy. Cheap. Guarded. Secretive. These are the characteristics of Sales "Pitchers". You know, those people who don't sell very much. So don't be that way. Be generous. Be open. Be willing to spend money to make money. Then you will meet more prospects and sell more stuff.

This is not to say you should be an endless source of generosity. You need to have a definitive end point to the free value. That's the key idea: You pile on the free value, and then it ends. At that point, the prospect has to say yes or no (more on that later).

That's what we do. We offer a free 90-minute coaching session called *The BIG Idea Outfitter*. It's our free value. We help people come up with their BIG Idea, package their elevator speech, and develop new marketing strategies—all for free. The session is extremely valuable. Another company might charge $5,000 for this service, but we do it for free because it attracts a lot of prospects. However, we don't do it for everyone. We carefully pick and choose who gets to do it. And most importantly, when the session is over, the prospect has to make a decision—yes or no. There is no maybe. A maybe is a no in my book. If they say no, the value ends. Pure and simple. If they say yes, the value continues. (More about this in Chapter 23).

But that's not how most Sales "Pitchers" do it. Because they don't provide any value until the person buys, the sales process tends to drag on indefinitely until the prospect is convinced they will get value for their money. That is what is ironic about the anti-free-value crowd. They actually give away a lot more free value, and they do it over an extended period of time.

I call this *Lazy Selling*. It is lazy because they haven't spent the time and effort to package what they are doing, or provide a package of free value. It's also lazy because they don't want to force the issue and ask for the sale. They delay the moment of truth.

In our program, we ask for payment upfront on a credit card. This is unheard of in our industry. Other marketers don't believe anyone will pay upfront for our kind of services. And yet we have closed hundreds of clients in the last 10 years, who have paid upfront more than 6,000 times. We make it work because we packaged our BIG Idea and provide tremendous free value that clearly demonstrates upfront the value of our work. That makes our prospects more willing to pay up front.

We've taught our clients to do the same thing. We've helped them package their BIG Idea and provide free value. Some of them provide 90 minutes of coaching. Some of them provide software or books or even trips to a spa. They do this because it's easier and it works better. It also attracts a lot more prospects.

In addition, providing free value helps you stand out in the crowd. Most of the penguins in your industry are Sales Pitchers. They will never provide any free value. They will just keep knocking on doors and giving their sales pitch. So if you provide free value, you will instantly stand out as different. You will no longer be a penguin in the eyes of your prospects.

So what could you provide as free value?

Chapter 22

Buying Bocce Balls:
Why Three is Better Than One

For some strange reason, I woke up one morning determined to buy bocce balls. I just had to have them. I figured they would cost about 30 bucks. After all, they are just balls, I thought. How much could they cost?

When I got to the store, I found the bocce balls. They had three kinds. There were children's bocce balls for $30, an adult package for $60, and a tournament kit for $120. I never anticipated that I would have a choice, but I felt empowered. After considering my options I chose the adult package for $60.

When I got home, I told my wife that I got the bocce balls (she was thrilled as you can imagine) and I explained that I had only spent $60, a real deal. "But you were only going to spend $30," she said, "How is that a deal?" I replied that I didn't really know how much they would cost, and anyway, I didn't spend $120. She wasn't buying it, but I thought my logic was sound. I was pleased with my consumer savvy.

This is the principle of *The Three Boxes*, as explained in my previous book *How To Sell A Lobster*. When you give your prospects three choices, most of them will choose the middle option, which is usually called the regular to denote that it is the most popular selection. This helps you up-sell prospects into a more expensive package, while making them feel empowered at

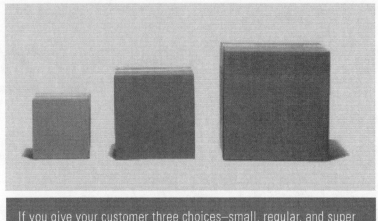

If you give your customer three choices—small, regular, and super size—they will feel empowered and buy more.

the same time. By packaging your BIG Idea into three boxes, you sell more, and sell bigger. As an added bonus, no one ever complains that you charge too much.

The typical penguin only offers one choice. But this just leaves a stark yes and no decision and most of the people will say no because that is the safer decision. But when you offer three choices, people will be able to say no to two options and then say yes to the middle, most popular choice.

By giving people choices, you take the heat off yourself, and put the focus on the prospect. Instead of them thinking you charge too much, or trying to haggle with you, they have to decide what kind of person they are: Are they a basic, regular, or super-size person? They have to decide what kind of self-image they want to have. It is all up to them to decide.

In most cases, I suggest the following. Make your existing penguin-style fast food offering the basic choice. Make your new, gourmet BIG Idea the middle, regular choice, and then create a super-size third choice that takes your BIG Idea to an even higher, perhaps even ridiculous level. Remember that you are not expecting anyone to buy your super-size. If they do, that's a bonus. It is really there to lead people to your new BIG Idea in the middle.

I love this strategy because it helps people spend the money required to get what they really need. It helps them stop being penny-wise and pound foolish. Too often we think everyone will only spend the least amount possible. But if that were true, we would all be driving the cheapest cars and wearing the cheapest clothes.

We are also afraid to raise our prices because we think we will lose sales. That would be true if we only had one choice and we increased the price too much. But this is a different approach. We give them a cheap option, and two more expensive options. But this doesn't mean they will always choose the cheapest one. In fact, they will go for the middle option 60% of the time on average.

The Three Boxes Strategy is great for two reasons. One, you make more money. But more importantly, by getting your customers to pay more, you are able to help them more. You can spend more time with them, and bring in more and better resources, all of which will help them get the results they really want.

So stop just selling one box. Sell three boxes. Everyone will benefit.

Chapter 23

No More Maybe World:
Creating A Sense of Urgency

Are you sick and tired of living in *The Maybe World*? That's when prospects tell you they "may" buy what you are selling. They just want to think about it. And you know what happens. Ninety-nine percent of the time they never come back. Their maybe was really a no. They were just too polite to say it.

That's why I insist that my prospects give me a clear yes or no at the end of my starter session. I'm not interested in a maybe. When I hear a maybe, I hear no, and I move on. I move on because I'm not interested in carrying around a *Bag of Hope*. That's a bag filled with maybes from prospects that you hope will one day turn into yes's.

I see a lot of penguins living in *The Maybe World* walking around with their *Bag of Hope*. They aren't out aggressively marketing because they have a bag of maybes that they hope will turn into sales. But they never do. They are just kidding themselves.

I don't give myself the luxury of maybes. I demand a yes or no. When I get a maybe, I move on and redouble my marketing efforts. I start looking for more new prospects. I keep looking for more yes's. I don't mind a no. At least that's clear and honest. I find maybes really annoying, and I don't put up with them anymore. I suggest you do the same.

Don't carry around a Bag of Hope. Create a sense of urgency by asking your prospects for a Yes or No.

I have another analogy that helps me: Red Light, Green Light. I am always looking for green lights: people who totally buy into what I'm doing. I'm also on guard for the first sign of a red light. As soon as I realize I've got a red light on my hands, I disengage. I move on. I don't waste even a second more on the red light. The same goes for a yellow light. For me, a yellow light is red.

Too many penguins spend their days standing at red lights. They work really hard trying to convince prospects to buy their widget. The more the prospect resists, the more they try to overcome that resistance. Meanwhile, they ignore all the green lights. That's why most penguins don't sell very much.

Don't be a penguin standing at red lights. Give yourself a break. Before you provide the free value, ask your prospects to promise a yes or no when the free value ends. Don't give them the free value if they don't promise a yes or no.

This strategy works well because it creates a sense of urgency. If the prospect knows they have to make up their mind, they will pay greater attention to what's going on. Because you are forcing the issue, and asking for the sale, your prospect picks up on this sense of urgency. It is now or never. The train is leaving the station. They have to decide right now if they want to get on or be left standing on the platform.

Giving up *The Maybe World* and putting down your *Bag of Hope* takes guts. You give up the false solace of hope for the clear certainty of success or failure. That's scary.

But you quickly realize that *The Yes-or-No World* is a happier and most prosperous place. You are no longer on an emotional roller-coaster. You feel more grounded and empowered. You are in charge.

This is the value of packaging your BIG Idea. The better the packaging, the easier it is for your prospects to say "yes" to what you are selling. There is no reason for them to say "maybe" because they are not sure what they are buying.

Imagine if everyone was skilled at asking for, and giving, a clear yes or no for every transaction. Imagine what that would do for our economy. Imagine what that would do for our society. As it is, our economy and our society are clogged up with maybes.

Life is too short to live in *The Maybe World*. Put down your *Bag of Hope*, and pick up a *Bag of Cash*.

Chapter 24

The Road of Good Intentions:
Observing The Ethical Imperative

They say the road to hell is paved with good intentions. I disagree. I believe good intentions are the most important thing we need to succeed in today's economy. It is also the primary motivation of *The Magnetic Marketer*.

You might think that some of the techniques suggested in this section are off-side. Some people have an ethical problem with The Line-up strategy for example. I get that. But I think the most important thing to consider in all of this is: What are your underlying intentions? Are you really trying to help people? Or are you just trying to sell something to people whether they need it or not? We have certainly seen the chaos created by companies that have had the wrong intentions. We've learned that the road to ruin—and sometimes jail—is actually paved with bad intentions.

So get clear about your intentions. Ask yourself some hard questions. Search your soul. Are your intentions good or bad?

This may sound a little flakey, but it is critically important. We live in a world that is becoming increasingly transparent. It's harder for people and companies to engage in bad business practices and get away with it. Word spreads quickly on the Internet. As they say, you can spend a lifetime building up your reputation, and a minute losing it. It's also hard to get it back once its gone.

I call this *The Ethical Imperative*. It is imperative that we have good ethical intentions. Otherwise, success will be elusive, and at best, unsustainable.

That's why I believe these Magnetic Marketing techniques, and those explained in my Lobster book, are so important. They might be a little unconventional, but if they are being used for a good cause, then they are okay. In this case, the end justifies the means.

I also believe it is important for us to have fun. Most penguins today are too serious. A serious demeanor stifles our creativity, and makes us sour-pusses. A serious mien doesn't help us make people feel better, and open our minds to new possibilities. Fun is better. When you and your customers are having fun, they are more creative and open minded. Things get done. Success happens.

So make sure you have good intentions, and have fun.

PART FIVE:

There Must Be Some Kind Of Way Out Of Here

Chapter 25

The BIG Idea Adventure:
Saying Goodbye To Your Penguin Friends

In Lord of The Rings, Frodo is given a terrifying task by the wizard Gandalf. He has to leave his home in The Shire, journey to Mordor, and throw The Ring into the fires of Mount Doom. Frodo, being a Hobbitt, doesn't want to do it. He would rather stay in Hobbiton and live out his days in peace and serenity. But he also knows that he, and everyone he loves, will face grave danger if he doesn't take up the adventure.

When it comes to our BIG Idea, many of us are reluctant heroes like Frodo. We have something we dream of doing, but we are afraid. The status quo, even if it is boring and unfulfilling, is also cozy and comfortable. The BIG Idea, while exciting, is scary. It can feel like a journey to Mount Doom.

I believe the fear you feel is a message. It is a message that your BIG Idea is the adventure you must take. If there is no fear, then it isn't your call to the adventure. Let me repeat that: If you feel fear about your BIG Idea, it's a good thing. It means it is the adventure that is waiting for you. If you don't feel any fear, it means your idea is the wrong one, or it isn't big enough.

For example, I'm not afraid to become a concert pianist. That's because I don't know how to play the piano, and really have no interest in it. But I'm afraid to write a novel. I'm afraid because it's something I dream of doing, and I could probably accomplish. My fear is a message that someday I should write a novel.

So see fear as a friend, and a teacher. It is telling you something. It is up to you to decide what it is telling you.

I can't think of anything sadder than people who never confront their fears. They have never listened to what life is asking of them. As a result, they live their whole lives in fear, never growing, or discovering what they are capable of.

As human beings, I believe we have a creative impulse that is always coursing through our being. In fact, I believe every creature in the universe has this impulse. It is what life is all about. It is what the universe is about. We are meant to keep changing and growing. Life is not about staying in the same place, doing the same things over and over again because it makes us feel safe. We were not meant to be penguins, all huddled together in the cold, staying in the same place year in and year out.

I've met many people who never embark on their adventure because they like having the dream more than achieving it. Many people come into our office and tell us about their fabulous BIG Idea. We get very excited for them, and start planning how they can achieve it. But then something strange happens. The person gets very uncomfortable. Sometimes they get angry or anxious. Sometimes they get depressed. They get this way because they don't really want to work on their BIG Idea, they just like thinking about it. They are afraid that if they work on it, it might be too hard, or it might not happen. Then they wouldn't have their pipe dream to carry around with them anymore.

Clinging to our fantasies is understandable, but it is also pathetic. There is a great play by Eugene O'Neill called *The Iceman Cometh*. It takes place in a downtrodden saloon and rooming house operated by owner Harry Hope. The large cast of characters is mostly alcoholics who spend their days regaling each other about their pipe dreams; the wonderful things they will do in the future. They take solace in these dreams, but they have no intention of ever working on them. They harbor the fear that if they work on their dreams they may never achieve them, and then all hope will be lost forever.

I meet people every day who carry around their pipe dreams. Over the years, these pipe dreams have become so near and dear to them that they are afraid to give them up by actually working on them. They would rather have dreams than face reality.

I see this a lot with people who say they want to write a book. I know many people who have been talking about writing a book for years. But they never sit down and write it. They would rather carry the book dream around with them rather than work on it.

I always say: There are two kinds of authors in the world: The authors who write books, and the authors who talk about writing books. The same goes for dreams: There are people who talk about their dreams, and there are people who work on their dreams.

Many people also feel trapped in their current situation. They say: "I want to work on my BIG Idea, but I can never find the time. I'm bogged down in my existing business. I don't have the energy to work on my BIG Idea." The list of excuses goes on and on. I've often remarked that if people put into their BIG Idea the energy they put into making excuses, they could achieve anything.

Another excuse people make about their BIG Ideas is that they don't know how to achieve their goal. I would like to produce a movie, but I don't know how. I would like to sail a yacht, but I don't know how. I would like to operate a bed and breakfast, but

Many of your penguin friends will try to stop you from pursuing your Big Idea.

I don't know how. There is some notion that we have to know exactly how to do something before we can start doing it.

This is silly. They didn't know how to get to the moon when President Kennedy made his famous speech about landing a man on the moon by the end of the 1960s. They set the goal and then they figured it out. I didn't know how to write a book when I wrote my first one in 1995. I just set the goal and figured it out as I went along.

Not knowing the path is part of the adventure. It's what makes it interesting. Embracing the unknown is what the adventure is all about. It's what makes it fun.

Probably the biggest obstacle to a BIG Idea is negativity from the other penguins. Consumed with their own fear, they will do everything they can to stop you from leaving the pack. They don't want you to succeed and show them up. They want to keep you drinking at Harry Hope's bar and grill.

I remember years ago I had a BIG Idea to start a magazine. I was young and ambitious, and I had no idea how to put together a magazine, but I really wanted to do it. One day, I was telling a neighbor about it, and he was very negative. "It will never work," he said. "There are too many magazines out there already." I walked away from the conversation feeling deflated and depressed. I was thinking about abandoning the whole idea, but my Mom saved me. She said: "Don't listen to him. He has never pursued any dreams in his life, and he doesn't want to see anyone achieve theirs. It would make him feel bad about himself."

My Mom was absolutely right. When you have a BIG Idea, there will be lots of penguins who will try to burst your bubble of enthusiasm. That's why it's important to pick your BIG Idea confidantes very carefully. Don't share your ideas with everyone. There is nothing wrong with wise sober counsel, but you want to speak with people who are committed to helping you achieve your BIG Idea, not scuttle it.

At our office, we have a rule about BIG Ideas. We have to give our budding ideas a chance to survive. Too often a BIG Idea is snuffed out before its tender shoots have had a chance. Someone comes up with an idea, and immediately, there are a dozen reasons why it can't be done. So we have a three-stage *BIG Idea Incubator.* When someone comes up with a BIG Idea, we put it in the incubator. In stage one, you are only allowed to talk positively about the idea itself. What it will look like and feel like. What it will be like to achieve it. What the benefits will be. Once the idea has been fully fleshed out—with enthusiasm— then we move to stage two. In this stage, we are only allowed to talk about how to achieve the goal. What resources and strategies will be used? Who will do what? No one is allowed to voice any criticism or talk about roadblocks. Only at stage three do we talk about any issues that we may need to overcome.

It doesn't mean that every BIG Idea is a good one. Some baby ideas look really cute, like a chick in an incubator, but they turn into a chicken when fully grown. But that's the whole point. We don't know which BIG Idea is good, so we have to nurture all of them to some extent. Sometimes a bad idea will lead to a good idea.

The point is to foster an environment for BIG Ideas, and not get caught up in the dark "failurism" of your fellow penguins. Accept that most of your fellow feathered friends will never leave their cozy ice floe. For them, the iceman has already cometh. You have to decide for yourself if you want to stay put, or if you want to follow your dream.

It's not easy to leave your buddies behind. They are your friends. But sometimes you have to say goodbye to the other penguins if you want to be happy. The other penguins will be sorry to see you go, but they will get over it.

Chapter 26

The New Factory:
Making The Transition To Your BIG Idea

Think of your existing business as your Old Factory. Years ago you had a BIG Idea to build this factory. You constructed the building, installed the machines, and assembled the staff to run it. Day by day, you honed and perfected the operations, and created a profitable company. Now as an established business, the factory churns out cash, and provides you with a comfortable living. You're very proud of what you've accomplished, but now you have a few problems.

For one, you've become bored with the business. You feel like it's "been there, done that." Although your skills and interests have changed, your business has not. The old factory was structured for you to exploit your old skills and interests, not your new ones. That's why you feel trapped. The business you spent years to create has become a prison that won't allow you to self-actualize.

This feeling is even more acute because you have a BIG Idea, something new, better, and different you want to do. The gulf between your deepest desire and your present reality makes you feel despondent. Perhaps you are even "living a life of quiet desperation," to quote Henry David Thoreau. Perhaps you fear you will "go to your grave with the song still in you."

Many people ensnared in this dilemma try to retool their old factory. They start changing their operations. They add new

Get your Big Idea off the ground by building your New Factory while still running your Old Factory.

machines, and new parts. They hire and fire staff. But it just doesn't work. In fact, it makes things worse because now the cow isn't pumping out the cash like it used to. So you revert back to your old factory ways and wallow in quiet desperation once again.

But it doesn't have to be this way. You can keep running your Old Factory while building your New Factory. Keep the Old Factory churning away, with its rusty old parts, while you go across the street and build a completely New Factory from scratch, with all brand-new parts.

At first, you might only have a few hours a week to spend on your New Factory. That's okay. At least you're working on your dream. You can still spend most of your time on your Old Factory in order to keep paying the bills. But now you won't mind toiling away at the boring Old Factory because you know it won't last forever.

I first used this trick when I was working at a corporate public relations company. I hated working there, and I dreamed about having my own business. But I had to keep paying the bills and I couldn't just quit my job. So I worked on building my New Factory in the evenings and on weekends. I set up the business in my apartment, and got a bunch of clients. After six months, my New Factory was up and running. Then I gave notice at work, and on my first day of full-time operation, my business was a going concern.

I also used this approach to get my coaching program started. About ten years ago, we were marketing "builders." We built marketing tools like brochures and websites. But I wanted to be a marketing "architect" and help people develop BIG Ideas.

To get this new business started, we simply carried on with our Old Factory, while building the New Factory. I began by offering my existing clients a free three-hour BIG Idea session. Twenty-five of them agreed, and I took them through my new process. From this experience I refined the steps and realized I could start charging for it. Gradually, I spent more and more time on this new program—The BIG Idea Adventure—and less time on my Old Factory. As of today, we've had more than 1,000 entrepreneurs go through the program, and the New Factory has become our main business.

It's important to remember The New Factory does not contain any parts from The Old Factory. You start with a blank slate and build exactly what you want. You don't bring over any of the old parts from the Old Factory. You keep it running the Old Factory as long as you like, until you've got the New Factory operational.

We've helped hundreds of people use this technique to break out of old structures and build new structures that empower them to live their dream.

So isn't it about time you started working on your New Factory?

Chapter 27

Rising and Passing Away:
Why You Will Always Need New BIG Ideas

Once you leave the penguin patch, there is no going back. Once you create a BIG Idea, and become a Magnetic Marketer, you won't want to go back. But you could fall into a trap. You could start clinging to your new BIG Idea and try to make it permanent.

But that's not how it works on *The BIG Idea Adventure*. Your BIG Ideas are not permanent. They are constantly arising and passing away. Today's BIG Idea will one day become an Old Idea. And then you will have to come up with a new BIG Idea and the cycle will continue.

Too many business people think taking risks is a one-time thing. They invest time and money in a new venture, and they hope that this idea will go on forever. Long after a period of success, they continue to push around a donkey cart carrying their old idea from two decades ago. They never think that maybe they need a new BIG Idea.

It would be great if we only needed one BIG Idea in our lifetime, but that's not how things work. Sorry. Best to adopt an attitude of continuous BIG Idea generation. You might never do them all, but you always stay open to new ideas. That's actually more fun, and can lead to some exciting places. So isn't it about time you stopped being a penguin, and started on your BIG Idea Adventure?

Want more penguin? Visit <u>www.BishopBigIdeas.com</u> for videos and updates.

PART SIX:

Tools For Penguins In Recovery

Suggested Additional Reading

Ariely, Dan, *Predictably Irrational*, HarperCollins Publishers: New York, 2008

Chan, Kim W., *Blue Ocean Strategy: How To Create Uncontested Market Space and Make Competition Irrelevant*, Harvard Business School Publishing Corporation: Boston, 2005

Danesi, Marcel, *Brands*, Routledge: Abingdon, UK, 2006

Godin, Seth, *All Marketers Are Liars: The Power of Telling Authentic Stories in a Low Trust World*, Penguin Books: New York, 2005

Jensen, Rolf, *The Dream Society: How The Coming Shift From Information To Imagination Will Transform Your Business*, McGraw-Hill: New York, 1999

Levitt, Theodore, *The Marketing Imagination*, MacMillan Inc: New York, 1983

Norman, David A., *Emotional Design: Why We Love Or Hate Everyday Things*, Perseus Book Group: New York, 2004

Pine, Joseph & Gilmore, James H., *The Experience Economy: Work Is Theatre & Every Business A Stage*, Harvard Business School Press: Boston, 1999

Pink, Daniel H., *A Whole New Mind: Moving From The Information Age to The Conceptual Age*, Penguin Books: New York, 2005

Tofler, Alvin and Heidi, *Revolutionary Wealth*, Borzoi, Random House: New York, 2006

West, Scott & Mitch, Anthony, *Story Telling For Financial Advisors: How Top Producers Sell*, Kaplan Publishing: Chicago: 2000

Glossary of Terms

Architect: A person who helps their customers develop Blueprints based on Models developed by Theorists.

Bag of Hope: When a salesperson or business owner foolishly hopes that a prospect that said 'maybe" will one day become a customer.

BIG Icon: A character or image that becomes representative of your business, such as Mr. Clean, the Goodyear Blimp or the Eveready Bunny.

BIG Idea: Something new, better and different that sets you apart from your competition, and gets you excited again about your business.

Branding: The combination of feelings and thoughts about your company in the hearts and minds of your customers.

Brand Name: The name given to your BIG Idea, such as *The Presto Pressing System.*

Builder: A person who works on Jobs as part of a Project coordinated by a Contractor.

Concept Tornado: A confusing whirlwind of ideas, concepts, symbols and models that make it difficult to clearly explain your business and what it does.

Contractor: A person who works on Projects based on Blueprints developed by Architects.

Design Map: A map used to pre-plan all design elements of your physical packaging.

Ethical Imperative: The need to have good intentions in order to succeed in today's economy.

Evocative Design: Physical packaging designed to evoke specific thoughts and feelings in your customers.

Fast Food Business: Companies that sell large volumes of products and services at low-margin prices to a large number of customers they don't know very well.

Free Value: Something of value offered for free to get more prospects to meet with you.

Gourmet Business: Companies that provide unique high-end products and services at premium prices to a select number of high-quality customers they know extremely well.

Green Light: A prospect who is completely open to, and excited about, what you are selling.

Laborer: A person who does a Task based on a Job managed by a Builder.

Lazy Selling: When a salesperson, who drags out the sales process, doesn't make the effort to definitively close prospects or get payment up-front.

Magnetic Marketing: Activities designed to attract your ideal customers and get them knocking on your door.

Maybe World: When a prospect says "maybe" when they really mean "no."

New Factory: The place, either real or conceptual, where you build and operate your new BIG Idea.

Number 1 Customer Type: The type of customer you really want to work with.

Old Factory: Your existing business that you keep running while you build your New Factory.

Packaging: The combination of ideas, words, images and experiences used to deliver your "brand" into your customers' hearts and minds.

Peak Benefit: The ultimate benefit, often overlooked, that your customers really desire.

Red Light: A prospect who you know deep down will never buy but you keep pursuing anyway.

Sales Pitcher: A salesperson who uses aggressive dynamic tactics to pitch their product or service to prospects.

Symbolspace: The intangible realm of concepts, ideas, models, and symbols which will become the dominant economic playing field of the 21st Century.

Theorist: A person who develops, packages and educates people about Models.

Three Boxes: Offering prospects three choices—small, regular, and super-size—in order to up-sell them.

Three C's: Three new benefits that companies can provide their customers: Caring, Coaching, and Coordination

Titanic Technique: A technique used to see the world through the eyes of your customers and develop new BIG Ideas that will be very valuable to them.

Transformation Economy: An economy based on doing everything possible to help people and companies transform their situation from out-of-shape to in-shape.

Transaction Economy: An economy based on doing transactions with customers with little or no regard for the ultimate positive or negative impact of that transaction.

Wal-Mart Effect: The negative impact on small businesses that are not willing to change when a large fast food competitor, such as Wal-Mart, prices them out of the market

Value Pyramid: A hierarchical model that delineates the different roles people play in the economy, from Theorist at the top to Laborer at the bottom.

Acknowledgements

I feel very fortunate to have the opportunity to write and publish a book like *The Problem With Penguins*. Although authorship can be a solitary endeavor, it is impossible without the support of many people who empower me to pursue my bliss. I begin by thanking my wife Ginny, whose contribution to my professional and personal growth is immeasurable. My kids Douglas and Robin have provided the kind of painfully honest advice and critiques only teenagers can deliver. My sister Diana, one of our BIG Idea coaches, who proves that BIG Idea blood runs in our family, has been a source of inspiration.

I would never be able to write any books if it were not for my friends and colleagues involved with The Big Group of Companies—Curtis Verstraete, Corey Kilmartin, Stephen Lindell, Sonia Marques, and Imran Mohammad. Their work with members of *The BIG Idea Adventure* has helped us develop many new concepts, ideas, and strategies that have found their way into this book.

I must also thank my agent Robert Mackwood for getting my books published around the world in many different languages. Without Robert, no one in Russia, China, Japan, India or Romania would have ever learned how to sell more lobsters or avoid the problem with penguins.

I would also like to thank the following clients and associates for their support: Jim Poe, Rick Bauman, Owen Smith,

Gregor Binkley, Martha Howard, Beverly Yates, Jim Bean, Jeff Calibaba, Jess Joss. John Brown, Katherine Bain, Mette Keating, Linda Robinson, Michael Wegener, Mitch Silverstein, Tina Tehranchian, Jason Greenlees, Stephanie Czachor, Jay Miller, Kelly Burnett, Janice Waugh, Jim Towle, Jody Silver, Malcolm Silver, Gary White, Scott Ford, John Durbano, Victor Matos, Wayne Baxter, Roch Beaulieau, Robert Young, Monika Pugliesi, Michael Pugliesi, Harold Agla, Bob Gould, Bob Kowaleski, Terry Ortynsky, Jim Gilbert, Jean-Luc Lavergne, Dawn Frail, Kelly Millar, Patrick Carroll, Garth Myers, Rick Borden, Rex Chan, Karla & Preston Diamond, Tim Yurek, Stuart Paris, Paul Reklaitis, Rob Geiger, Larry Trapani, Steven Stramara, Dean D'Camera, Adrian Davis, Doug McPherson, Ricky Lyons, Jon Singer, Al Singer, David Singer, Andy Wimberly, Alex Nicholson, Tom Miller, Marianne Cherney, Byron Woodman, Romy McPherson, Ben Darwin, Gair Maxwell, Mark Cupp, Kathleen Fry, Claudio DiSante, Darren Woodcock, Byron Meier, Tyler Trute, Doug Edwards, Larry Hamilton, Dan Millar, Brian Seim, Raymond Rupert, David Cohen, Stephanie McCullough, Harold Mertin, Greg Barnsdale, Wendy Kellar, and Dora Vell.

I would also like to thank the thousands of readers who have sent me e-mails from around the world explaining how they've used the strategies and concepts in my previous books. I appreciate your kind words and support. I love hearing from you.

THE BIG IDEA ADVENTURE
GET HELP WITH YOUR BIG IDEA

If you would like help with your BIG Idea, we offer a free Starter Session called The BIG Idea Outfitter. During the session you will:

- Clarify your vision for the future of your business.
- Identify your #1 Customer Type, and your Ideal Customer profile.
- Articulate the three fundamental Peak Benefits you provide (from the perspective of your customers).
- Determine new value you can provide to help your customers achieve their Peak Benefit.
- Develop a BIG Idea: something new, better, and different, that will provide

and differentiate you in the marketplace.

- Package this BIG Idea with a brand name and an elevator speech.
- Learn how you can use your BIG Idea to achieve your full potential.

The 90-minute BIG Idea Outfitter Session is provided free-of-charge to qualified candidates. To book your session, call **416.364.8770** or email **bill_bishop@biginc.com**. You can also visit **www.bishopbigideas.com**

HOW TO SELL A LOBSTER

HOW TO SELL A LOBSTER: THE UNCONVENTIONAL MONEY-MAKING SECRETS OF A STREETWISE ENTREPRENEUR.

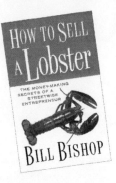

Are you looking for new ways to have fun and make more money? Are you searching for innovative and perhaps unconventional ways to get new ventures started or to create a bigger and better business? If so, *How To Sell A Lobster* is the perfect book for you.

Based on more than three decades of experience, streetwise entrepreneur Bill Bishop takes you on a hilarious and insightful adventure across the often weird but wonderful business landscape. With the help of his trusted mentor Marketing Mike, Bishop offers innovative approaches, special techniques, and proven strategies that will help your business develop big ideas, reach new customers, make a sale, and turn a profit.

Each chapter is a parable about a real-life business problem: learn how Bishop won a waiter contest by selling more than 1,400 lobsters; discover how to get a new venture started by overcoming The First-Member Trap; and find out how to increase your sales and profit margins by using The Three Boxes marketing game. Bold action and understanding what makes people tick; these are just some of the unconventional money-making secrets Bill Bishop reveals in this book.

To order, go to **www.amazon.ca** or call **416.364.8770 or visit www.bishopbigideas.com**

STAY CONNECTED WITH BILL
BIG IDEAS TO SELL MORE AND BE HAPPY

BILL BISHOP

CALL ME

If you want to contact me, call my office @ 416.571.8520 or 416.364.8770 X222

MY EMAIL ADDRESS

My email is: bill_bishop@biginc.com

VISIT MY WEBSITE

www.bishopbigideas.com

On my website, you will find free content from my books, audio CDs, speeches, videos, podcasts and blogs.

CATCH ME ON THE TUBE

I am always posting videos to YouTube from my speeches and workshops. Watch for my regular iPhone uploads direct from my workshop locations.

JOIN FACEBOOK GROUP

We have a group on Facebook called Bishop BIG Ideas. If you're on Facebook, join today.

@BISHOPBIGIDEAS

Got the Twitter bug? Follow me on Twitter @BishopBIGIdeas. I'l keep you posted on any BIG Ideas from me and my clients.

BIG IDEA BLOG

Stay motivated and informed by subscribing to my Blog on my website. I will be posting a blog once a week (unless on holidays).

LINK IN TO BIG IDEAS

Join my network at Linkedin. Send an invitation to me and I will connect with you.

BIG IDEA PODCAST

Subscribe to my PodCast and hear monthly (at least) audio advice about how to sell more, a lot more.To subscribe go to www.bishopbigideas.com.